Contents

Older Babies (over 6 months)

Toddlers and Older Children

Acknowledgements

This **Right from the Start** book is based on the practical experience of many parents, midwives and health visitors and on seven years of research and practice undertaken by Dr Richard Ferber at the Centre for Paediatric Sleep Disorders at The Children's Hospital, Harvard University, Boston, USA.

My warmest thanks go to Liz Marsden and Janet Watts, both health visitors working in Norwich, and to Yolanda Koning, a childcare teacher in Holland. The sleep clinic that Liz and Janet set up at the Lawson Road Health Centre, the details of their work and the help they have given to hundreds of desperately tired parents have been the clearest inspiration for this book.

I would also like to thank Dr Helen Ball, Director of the Parent/Infant Sleep Research Project at the University of Durham; Dr Alan Heath, Paediatric Surgeon, Queen Mary's, Carshalton and Southgates Medical and Surgical Centre, King's Lynn; Mary Obiamadi at the Community Practitioners and Health Visitors Association; Tazneen Khan at the Coram Family Parenting Centre and Kathryn Borg for her dreamtime story-telling experiences. Yvonne Aycliffe and Peggy Corney gave me the chance to watch and learn about the value of cranial osteopathy for babies and young children. The generous help of all these people is greatly appreciated.

My own energy in writing this book came in great measure from the many parents who are themselves at the heart of every page. I salute them with affection and gratitude.

For all her encouragement and for writing the foreword to this book my heartfelt thanks go to Angela Henderson.

For wonderfully careful and inspired editing I thank Jamie Buxton, Liane Jones, Claudine Whiting and Barbara Potter.

And finally I would like to say a special thank you to the parents and grandparents who donated photographs of their children, and shared with us their stories.

Sarah Woodhouse

Picture credits

All the drawings were done by Tim Baker, artist and actor.

Photographs were taken by:

Sally and Richard Greenhill, Anthea Sieveking, Le Boyer, Sandra Lousada, Fiona Pragoff, Roy Gumpel, Clive Harrison, Peter Cade, David Harrison (cranial osteopathy photograph) © Tatler/ Conde Nast Publications Ltd., Getty Images, Raven Cozens-Hardy, Charlie Bryan, Rosie Ferguson, Philip Green, Alban Donohoe, Laura Gould, Parents and Grandparents.

'Have you ever met a new baby before?'

Foreword

Congratulations! Reading this book will help ensure that the arrival of your new baby will be what it should be: one of the most joyful and fulfilling experiences of your life.

However, the joy of a new baby's arrival is often compromised for parents by the experience of having their much-loved infant screaming repeatedly in the middle of the night (often for nights on end), while they themselves are desperate for sleep, feeling overwhelmed by the sense of this new responsibility and simply unable to understand the reasons for their baby's sleeplessness. In the worst cases, when sleeplessness and crying go on for extended periods, confusion, exhaustion, a sense of failure and even ill-health can threaten a family's very stability and happiness. At times like this we long for the help and advice of our own mothers or grandmothers; someone who has seen it all before, is unworried by what is happening and who can offer us really solid advice. For those who want 'in-depth' advice for both babyhood and beyond, this book is the next best thing: in these pages Sarah Woodhouse brings us the sense of a reassuring, authoritative, motherly friend who can either guide us through, or better still help to prevent, such a situation. With observations from both western and eastern cultures, this invaluable book contains a wealth of information for all stages of your child's development. If you feel too exhausted to read the whole book, dip in instead to the relevant section for your child's age group and use the 'in a nutshell' summaries at the end of each section.

Psychologists recognise that most baby sleep problems are potentially avoidable – and that is why this book is so important. Whether or not your child develops sound sleeping habits is not just down to him or her – it is also up to you! How we parents interact with our babies in the early months, the routines we establish, the environment we create and how we learn to understand and respond to their cries, are all absolutely crucial in shaping relationships with our children and helping them develop good sleeping patterns – which in turn will ensure good rest and health through the rest of their childhood, and even into adulthood.

In researching and writing in this field myself I have found that one of the biggest mistakes made by new parents is to continue using into older babyhood a settling or soothing strategy that was right and natural for a newborn baby. It is easy to fear 'upsetting the apple cart', or become over-anxious about your baby crying. As this book explains, actually soothing your older baby to sleep can deprive her of the opportunity to learn to put herself to sleep. Another common mistake is lack of consistency. Once a strategy is adopted, it is important not to chop and change it on a nightly basis! Adopt an attitude of calm, consistent determination and you will succeed – your child can tell if you are confused, and this makes her feel less secure in turn. Finally, if you are at the end of your tether, don't be too proud to seek help (see the excellent resource section at the end of this guide). Health Visitors are a marvellous resource – let them help and support you too.

It is my sincere hope that, with the help of this book, your experience of parenting will be greatly enriched.

Angela Henderson
Author, *The Good Sleep Guide for You and Your Baby*

Introduction

This book is about how to understand your baby's crying and respond to it. It is also about how to settle babies, toddlers and young children and help them sleep.

The early chapters look at why babies cry, what it might mean and how you can comfort them. It is never *wrong* for a baby or child to cry. When they cry, they need to cry. It is their way of communicating with us. For a baby, crying is as natural as breathing and sucking. It is meant to break into our thoughts and attract our attention. It is up to us to accept the crying and offer help. But this is far from easy. What does the baby want? Why do some babies go on crying even after we have fed them, burped them, changed them and cuddled them?

This book looks at crying and screaming both from the baby's point of view, and from that of the parents and carers – what does this crying do to us? How can we help ourselves as well as our babies? It offers insights, tips, tactics and remedies drawn from the experiences of parents and professionals, helping you compare your experiences with other people's, and try out different things for calming and settling your baby.

A newborn baby is full of courage, and the longing to be loved and to love back. Giving birth and caring for your baby, and watching her grow and develop can be one of the most magical wonders in your life. The purpose of this book is to help make this so, through sharing ideas and offering encouragement.

Later chapters of the book focus on toddlers and older children. Learning how to settle themselves and sleep through the night is important for children's future health and happiness.

Every baby is different. Every child changes as it grows. Every experience of being a parent is unique. Put aside those parts of the book that don't suit you. Like clothes on a rack, find what fits and feels comfortable. Choose what is right for you and your child.

In order to avoid the awkwardness of using 'he or she' throughout the book, we have chosen to use 'he' in one chapter and 'she' in the next.

New Babies

(up to six months)

CHAPTER 1

Calming and Helping a Baby to Sleep

In this chapter we will look at your new baby's need for sleep and explore ways to soothe him to peacefulness and sleep, helping him get used to his new world. We will look at ways to begin to introduce a day and night rhythm, which will help everyone in the family to get the rest they need.

How much will a new baby sleep and when?

Newborn babies usually sleep deeply for about sixteen hours a day. They may sleep more during the first week if the exhausting adventure of being born, learning to breathe, and finding a breathing rhythm has tired them out. The rest of the time is spent sucking, with little cries now and again as they try to cope with the newness of everything and get used to the light and the faces around them.

Gradually, usually some time between 2 and 6 months, the hours a baby sleeps will slip down to about fourteen, and more of that sleep will be at night. But the variations between babies can be enormous.

Just occasionally – and it's very rare – a baby is born with much less need or less ability to sleep than normal. This can be tough for parents.

There is no settled pattern at first

A newborn baby has lived in the dark for nine months, waking and sleeping, wriggling and lying still, just as he feels like, without knowing the difference between night and day. So things are bound to be chaotic to begin with, until life after birth falls into some kind of clearer shape.

After a week or two most babies settle into the habit of longer and deeper sleeps between feeds during the night, and more wakefulness and alertness during the day. This happens as they come to feel the contrast between silent, barely-awake parents attending to their needs quite swiftly in near-darkness at night; and being surrounded, when they are awake in the light of day, by all kinds of absorbing sights, sounds and sensations. They stare and stare at smiling faces, especially those of their own parents. They gaze in fascination at bright objects and at colours, which they now begin to see as their eyesight develops. They hear familiar and new voices loudly and clearly now, and the clatter and stir of the day. Only slowly, as they gradually become more aware of daytime activities and begin to join in, will their day begin to separate from night.

As this contrast between day and night becomes greater, babies tend to move slowly into a pattern of sleeping for about four or five different periods, with two-thirds of this sleep being at night. By 6 to 8 months most babies have settled into a pattern, and sleep for about twelve hours each night, with waking and disturbance now and again. This is not necessarily a smooth process, however. With some babies the early months can seem like a whirlpool of unpredictability. This can be a difficult time for parents, so helping your child develop a regular sleeping pattern will ensure that both you and your child get much-needed rest and peaceful times.

Soothing your baby to sleep

Most of us spend the first six months practising all kinds of gentle, soothing ways to calm, relax and help our babies to sleep. The aim in the end, of course, is to enable your baby to put himself to sleep. However, during the first weeks and months he will need your help again and again during the day and probably in the night as well. When your baby reaches that half-year milestone, it is wise to begin slowly weaning him off soothing methods at sleep time so that he does not become dependant on you to get to sleep. But the soothing techniques described here to help a tiny baby sleep can still be used later on for relaxation, closeness and fun, or as part of the pre-bedtime routine.

Every baby is different. Things that may soothe one baby and help him sleep may stimulate another baby. So choose a few options that feel right for you and your baby, and try them out and see. If they do not seem to be working, try something else. The aim is to find out what is right for *you* and *your* baby. There is no right or wrong way.

Once you have found some solutions that work for you, try to establish a pattern that can be followed every day when it is time to sleep. This repetition will help give your baby a sense of security, of knowing what is coming next, and will help him understand that sleeping is just another part of his day. He will grow to know what to expect, and what is expected of him. For instance, if you choose to rock your baby to soothe him into sleep, he will begin to associate the rocking motion with sleep. The rocking movement would then become a 'trigger' to help

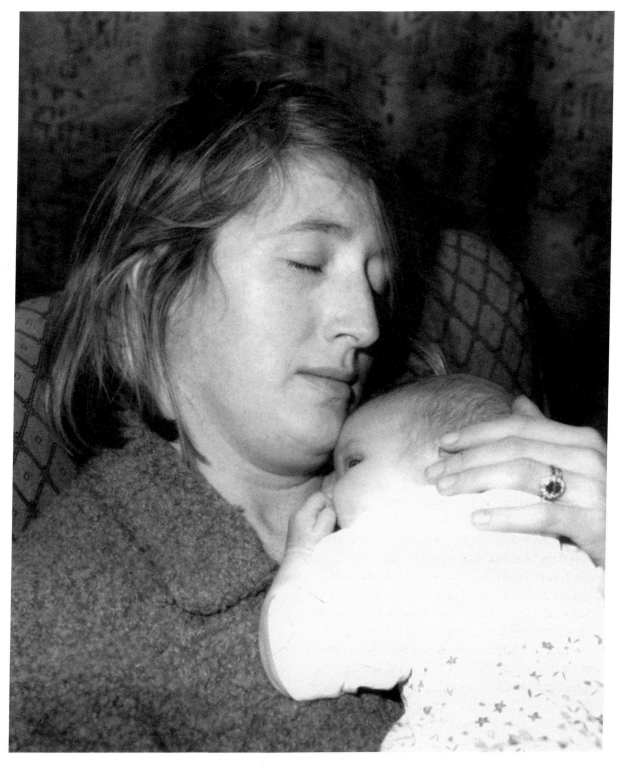

'Much needed rest even for a few minutes'

your baby sleep. If you can establish such sleep triggers you are well on your way to a healthy sleep pattern. Problems can start when a parent keeps on and on trying different things in an effort to find *just the right* solution. There is then a confusion of signals and little chance that a soothing method can become a sleep trigger. Often it is consistency that is needed rather than the perfect solution.

Soothing methods to try

- Allow him to suckle
- Stroke his head, tummy or legs with your fingertips in gentle, regular movements
- Darken the room
- Put a ticking clock near him – to remind him of your heartbeat
- Tuck him up well – like being back in the womb

> It is often easier to relax and pacify a crying baby if you are on your own with him. A second person anxiously hovering can make matters worse. If you are lucky enough to have help, either from your partner or from someone else, taking it in turns for a time can be better than doing everything together, and gives one of you a rest.

- Try rocking him to sleep
- Carry him around in your arms, walking at a steady pace
- Sing to him or play soft, lilting music

Let's look at some of these in more detail:

Sucking and sleep go hand-in-hand for most babies

Sucking comes completely naturally to babies – they do a lot of it even before they are born. Most babies literally suck themselves into drowsiness and sleep. Even if they don't suck themselves right to sleep, they suck themselves into contentment and peace. This happens because the action of sucking anything – whether milk is the outcome or not – stimulates the part of a baby's brain which secretes special chemicals called endorphins. Endorphins calm the baby and reduce stress and pain.

Sucking at his mother's breast is the best sucking of all for a baby, though this may not always be possible. Bottles, dummies and knuckles will do fine too! The bent knuckle of your little finger is just the right size and shape. Babies will need the comfort and the sustenance of sucking at regular and frequent times right through the day and the night for their first few months.

The importance of touch

For nine months, a baby has been totally encircled by his mother, feeling every movement she has made; and, during the last four months, hearing every word she has spoken, every beat of her heart and every trickle and rumble and surge of her circulatory and digestive systems.

Until birth, a baby has never experienced a single moment of complete silence or stillness, nor felt a rough texture or hard surface or cold air. No wonder he may sometimes feels sudden panic when he wakes up and finds there is silence, and nothing around him but dry sheets instead of that velvety, wet softness of the womb.

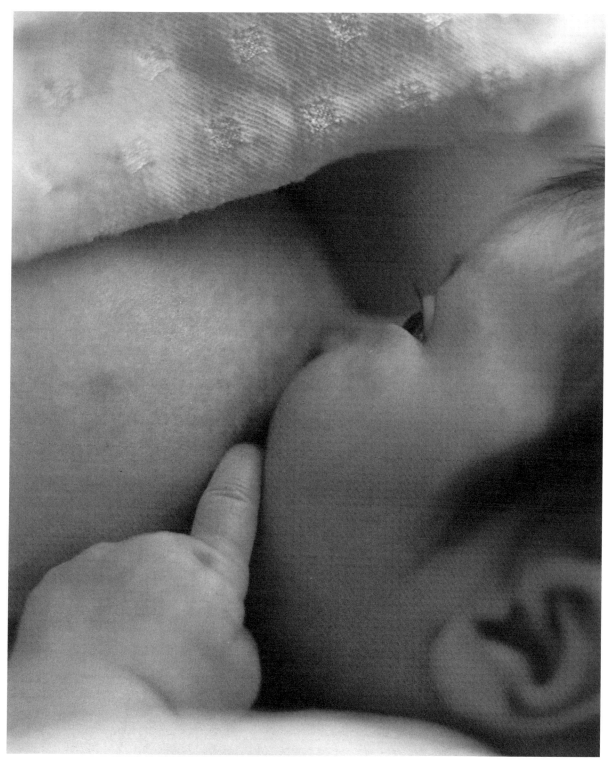

'Sucking himself into contentment and peace'

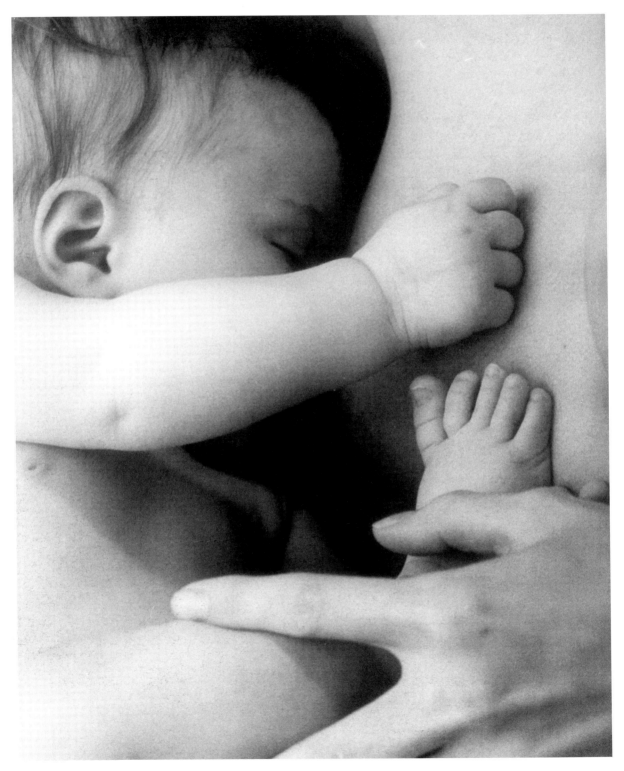

'The importance of touch'

His only means of communicating his distress is to cry. He is crying for touch and movement and to hear your voice. Skin-to-skin contact and gentle rubbing and stroking can make a big difference to a young baby's happiness.

Baby massage

You might want to learn how to massage your baby as a way of answering his need for touch. Massage is just a more precise and rhythmic way of extending the natural stroking and handling of a baby. It can bring great peace to a child and builds an especially close bond between the parent and child, which is not easily lost later. Many midwives and health visitors nowadays are trained to teach mothers how to do this. There are also books available on the subject. See the *Useful Books* list at the end of this book.

'How can you know you are alive if no-one touches you?'

Maureen Blackmore,
a nurse from Scunthorpe, Lincs.

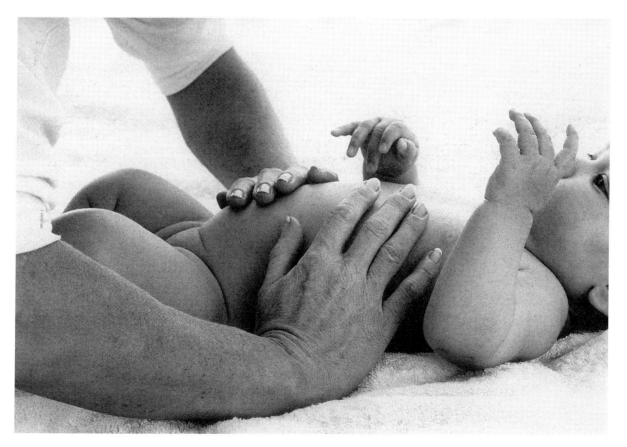

'Baby massage'

'Her touch. Her breath on my face. Her special smell.'

Dr Michel Odent, author of *Primal Health*, suggests that when you stroke a baby's skin this gives energy to the brain at an important stage in its development. He also describes in the book how babies will grow more understanding, sensitive and affectionate if they experience love through being touched, stroked and cuddled by their parents as often as possible. He believes that they will be more likely to become wonderful lovers and more able to build strong and lasting relationships when they grow up. They will also be less likely to suffer aches, pains and illness later in life.

In the mid 1990s, an advertisement was put in the *New York Times* appealing to nearby business men to give an hour of their time in the children's ward of one of the city's busiest hospitals – on their way home from work in the evening.

The nurses were desperate for help with caring for the ever-increasing number of babies born to drug-addicted mothers. Once born, these babies were suffering the torment of drug-withdrawal symptoms and screaming with the pain of it during their waking hours.

The only way their distress could be eased at all was to be held and carried around for an hour at a time.

The response to the advertisement was extraordinary. Immediately and continuously, teams of 'stand-in dads' arrived in the ward, coats off, sleeves rolled up, ready to pick up 'their' babies and start walking. Everyone's life was changed for the better.

Kangaroo closeness

After birth, baby kangaroos live in their mother's pouch, snuggled against her almost all day and night. Mothers and fathers can do the same! Kangaroo closeness is very soothing and helps tensions fall away. Here's one way to do it:

Lie yourself back, really comfortably, and then lay your baby on his front, on your bare chest, with nothing on him but a nappy. Just enjoy some time of peace together. Or use a babysling under a loose shirt to hold him in place if you need to walk about.

If a baby is held close in this way, the good feelings of velvety safety will come back to him, and the outside world will seem a less lonely and awkward place to be.

Your special smell

Some parents put a piece of soft clothing that they have worn and not yet washed, into their baby's bed so they can have a familiar smell close by even when left alone to sleep. It is a good idea to choose a t-shirt or vest so that it can be stretched over the mattress to prevent the baby becoming entangled or pulling the material up over his face.

Back-to-the-womb comforts

A baby is used to the dark. In fact, a break from the bright lights and colours of the new world and a little time spent in womb-like darkness may be soothing for him. So, try darkening the room. And, if it feels right to you, try placing a ticking clock nearby to remind him of the beating of your heart.

The womb was a warm place and very cramped. Your baby was curled up tight inside you and it will be new and strange for him to feel his limbs free and spread out. Though he may enjoy this new freedom, it can be comforting for the baby to sometimes feel held more snugly as he was in the womb, particularly when it is time to rest. You can do this by swaddling the baby, or using a sleeping bag, or simply by tucking in his sheets and blankets well. Swaddling is designed for newborns to four weeks old, and should be done with care to avoid overheating. (Please see appendix at the end of this book for more information on the benefits and risks of swaddling). Carrying baby in a sling-type carrier can also give him a sense of being 'cocooned' close to you.

Sleeping bags are now widely available and can be particularly useful for a baby who tends to kick off his covers at night. A chilly baby will be a wakeful one. A sleeping bag can also provide peace of mind if you are concerned that your baby may pull the covers up over himself in the night, or wriggle down under them.

During winter nights some parents keep their waking, hungry baby waiting for just long enough to fill a hot water bottle to put into the cot as they lift their baby out for a night feed. Slipping him back afterwards into a ready-warmed nest is more likely to lull him instantly back to sleep. *Be sure to take the bottle out before putting the baby back into bed.*

A baby in the womb is surrounded by the rhythms of his mother's body, close to the steady beating of her heart and the swing of her hips as she walks, feeling her body at rest and in motion. When a baby is born, he is used to being surrounded by all sorts of rhythms and can feel quite lost without them. Mimicking the rhythms of the womb can be very soothing to a baby. In the same way that a ticking clock placed near his bed can remind him of the sound of his mother's heartbeat, the rhythmic motion of the rocking chair can echo the sensation he felt inside his mother as she walked around.

Singing and music

Singing while you hold, rock or massage your baby or while you rub your child's back does something very special for you both. Your own voice singing lullabies, chanting rhymes, crooning and humming to your baby has a wonderfully calming influence. Nothing can beat it. It brings the baby not only the soothing melody of a familiar song, but also the comfort of hearing your voice. Remember that a baby doesn't mind whether you are a 'good' singer or not. Hearing your voice, the voice he has heard before birth and beyond, is what will soothe him, not the quality of the voice. You are the best music for your baby and you may be surprised that your song may soothe him in a way that even the most beautiful tape or CD cannot.

There are also physiological reasons why the sound of your singing voice gives your baby safe and warm feelings. The vibration of singing is different from the vibration of talking. It reaches parts of our brain that talking cannot touch. Singing can help us cope with physical difficulties and with emotional tension. It is part of being a human being and can give us a greater feeling of belonging to a larger community of people and peoples. Making music and singing together can rescue children, and perhaps society in general, from mistrust, fear and crime. Singing to our babies is the start of something big!

Music in the womb

During the last three months in the womb, babies hear sounds very clearly because the amniotic fluid surrounding them leads right into their ears and the fluid carries the sounds directly to their eardrums. People often think that if they sink their own head under water they will hear as the baby heard in the womb. This is not so. If we go underwater, a bubble of air gets trapped in the ear tube and cuts out some of the clarity. A baby in the womb actually hears much more clearly than we can underwater.

Music you enjoyed during your pregnancy could well have given your unborn baby the same feeling of relaxation and pleasure as it gave you. As you relaxed, he relaxed. Perhaps there was a song you sang again and again, or a piece of music you played many times. These sounds will have gone so deep during his time in the womb that they may continue to relax and soothe him after birth. It's worth a try and will be enjoyable for you too.

What your baby hears of your singing voice will not only comfort and quieten him after he is born, but will also be a lasting memory, tucked away but able to surface again once he is old enough to speak and sing himself. It may all come back when you least expect it.

Where to start?

Most people instinctively want to sing to their babies but it can be difficult knowing how to start. Sometimes self-consciousness or not having the words or the tune of a song ready in our heads holds us back. We learn by listening to the same tune again and again until its shape is in our heads strongly enough for us to take a breath and copy it. See the Music, Riddles and Rhymes section at the end of this book for books, tapes or CDs to help you learn songs.

Most people find that they have inside themselves one or two musical sounds that feel exactly right and are easier to sing strongly and well than other notes. By finding songs that repeat our 'best' note or notes and singing them more often, we can discover that those singing sounds do something for us as well as for our babies. The vibration of these tones can relax and steady us.

Playing simple musical instruments can have a marvellous effect on young babies and children – and you don't need to be a musician to do it. Even if you have no musical training or have never

> I bought a lyre for my baby before she was even born. I played to her at night just before going to sleep. When she was newborn, it was amazing to see how relaxed she became when I played to her at bedtime. It was like she remembered. She would go really still and just listen. Now she is a toddler, everyone in the house gets serenaded – visitors, the dolls, even the dog.
>
> *Fred*

picked up an instrument before, you can improvise, perhaps on a recorder, a lyre or a xylophone. Just playing notes as they come to you can mesmerise your baby, and be relaxing for you too. As your baby grows he may well develop a fondness for the instruments you have played to him and will probably want to experiment with playing them too. Playing music together can be a wonderful experience for parents and children to share as part of family life. A few notes played on a simple instrument can be the start.

A music teacher in a London school told her friends how one of the best times of her life had been living in Indonesia when her husband was working in Jakarta. They were newly married and expecting their first child. They lived in a hill village not far from the city. All the women in the village taught her Indonesian songs while they scrubbed and rinsed out their clothes and linen together in the wash tank in the market square. One song they taught her, a love song, was so beautiful that she sang it again and again every day all through her pregnancy. It became her own theme song. She played the tune on her flute too.

Two weeks before their baby was due to be born her husband was suddenly recalled to London and they had to leave Indonesia immediately. She completely stopped singing the Indonesian songs she had learnt. She was missing her life out there so much that she realised that singing anything in Indonesian would only make her feel more upset at having to leave. They just had to begin a very different life in London.

One morning a few years later their little daughter was alone, sitting in the sandpit in the sun outside the kitchen window. She was very quiet and peaceful. Her mother was inside, out of sight, standing by the window. Suddenly she heard the three year old starting to sing just a few notes at first and then adding others and continuing to sing more and more clearly. In amazement, she found herself listening to the Indonesian love song that had meant so much to her. The child sang it from beginning to end, a song she must have heard many hundreds of times before her birth but never once since.

Night-time

Your baby's needs at night

It's dark. It's quiet. Your body tells you it's time to sleep … unfortunately the same can't be said for your baby. In their first few months, babies wake and open their eyes in the night more fully and often than older children and adults. It's natural for them at that age. They expect to find you there!

Newborn babies sleep for a few hours, wake and feed, then sleep again, in a continuous cycle,

In *Set Free Childhood,* author Martin Large has the following to say about the effects of more chaotic, or electronic, noises in the home:

Babies' ears are easily damaged. They are very sensitive to noise. They become restless and edgy if there is constant background noise from TV, videos, radios and sound systems. They may react by crying, attention-seeking – or even shutting off. Some even react by going into a restless sleep as a defence against loud electronic noise. The noisier the home, the more sleep problems there may be. Babies need a calm, peaceful home, especially a quiet place to sleep.

Dr Sally Ward is a speech therapist from Manchester who tested 1000 children; first when they were nine months and then when they were two. She found that a quarter of the children who came from very noisy homes had serious listening and speech problems. It took longer for them to learn to talk (Andrew Hobbs, *Observer*, 1st August 1993). She recommends calming the home by turning down the volume or switching off, and by a parent taking time to play and speak with their baby or child over bath and bedtimes.

So one thing you can try if your baby or child has sleep problems is to firstly take stock of noise levels at home. You may be surprised at how much there is! Then, see what happens to your baby's ability to sleep by switching off or turning down the radio or TV. And try switching off altogether an hour or two before nap and bedtimes – with a song, story or game your child likes playing. See what changes happen!

day and night. Breast-fed babies sometimes begin to sleep for longer periods at around five days old when their mother's milk begins to flow in abundance, but by and large the waking-feeding-sleeping cycle will continue for at least the first eight weeks of life. Although, after two months, your baby will gradually begin to sleep for longer periods at night, he will still be awake fairly regularly in the night, following his own pattern as often as not. Change is seldom smooth. He may start to sleep for five or six hour periods at night, only to revert suddenly to a spate of nights when three-hour sleeps and ravenous feeds make you think you've been catapulted back to square one.

Your needs at night

Each of us has our own individual sleep needs and habits. It usually takes about three weeks to change any habit – in this case to get used to being woken up again and again in the night and then getting back to sleep again quickly. You may need to develop a new habit of having a catch-up sleep sometime during the day, if that is feasible. Try sleeping when your baby sleeps, particularly if you have not got anyone to take over for you while you have a nap. It could take a little getting used to, particularly if you have been a very active person who is not accustomed to napping – but this is not laziness, this is survival!

Most new mothers find it hard to imagine or make plans for coping with night-time waking. They may also feel anxious about the lack of sleep they will soon experience. If you are reading this book before the birth of your baby, it is worth thinking it out in advance and having some ideas at the ready.

Forced waking in the middle of the night sends a rush of adrenalin into our systems and our heart rate goes up. This is an exhausting experience until we learn to accept it and handle it calmly. To minimise exhaustion:

- Have everything ready to hand if you are bottle-feeding, including a bottle-warming method – maybe a filled electric kettle or thermos and a bowl.
- Make yourself very comfortable while breast-feeding, either lying in bed or sitting in a soft chair with cushions.
- If you have a partner or someone else to help you, try to take turns at night with bottle-feeding and comforting. You may find it best to do whole alternate nights on duty for a while.
- If you are breastfeeding, consider expressing some milk so that someone else can feed the baby sometimes. A good night's sleep will certainly do you good and if it is Dad who's doing the feeding, a little father-and-baby bonding is always a good thing.

To begin with, I used to jerk awake at the first loud cry of the night as if someone had thrown a bucket of water over me. My heart would still be banging against my ribs minutes later, even though Josh was now in bed with me and sucking peacefully. His 3 am feed, as often as not at 2.15 am, would mean another heart-banging session, and the dawn screams three hours later for his breakfast would give me the worst jerk of all as I was usually even more deeply asleep at that time.

I tried all sorts of ways to calm myself down and get myself back to sleep again quickly. Probably your own ideas work best because only you know yourself, however mine were: singing 'Here – I – come – Josh' inside my head as a four note tune as I slowly got out of bed and walked to pick him up from his cot. Or I rubbed my hands over my whole face and head, especially my forehead, as I walked to him. That felt surprisingly comforting, and my heart rate began to slow down. Or I would kiss his hand or the top of his head more and more slowly as he suckled. It was as if my mouth and his mouth were the two bridges between us, and he was giving me his contentment and peace. After a few weeks, even if the waking up was still hard, it stopped shaking me up so much. Feeding Josh during the stillness of the night became more of a treat and less of a trial.

Lisanne

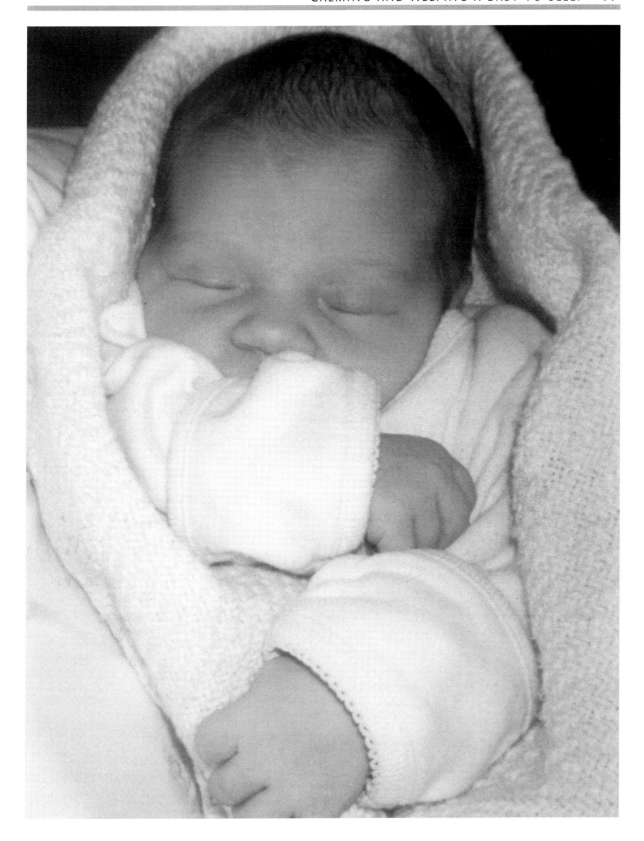

A bedtime routine

Developing a bedtime routine or rhythm, and following it each evening, is the first step towards helping your baby understand the difference between day and night and helping him settle into sleep. The process takes time and patience, but eventually your baby will come to associate his bedtime routine with the long sleep of night-time.

Below is Christina's description of the difficulties she had settling her sixteen-month-old baby and how success only came when she developed a simple and steady bedtime routine.

I was breast-feeding Chloe and would feed her each night lying down until she fell asleep. This often took ages, sometimes two hours to settle her. As long as I was lying next to her, she was happy, and since I was tired from the birth, I didn't mind a bit. Sometimes we would both fall asleep like that and she would sleep in my bed for the whole night. But as time went on, I wanted to have some time in the evenings with my husband and began to feel a bit stuck upstairs feeding and feeding the baby, and I think she picked that up. Going to bed started to be stressful for her, she never knew what to expect, except that I was always anxiously waiting for her to fall asleep. Something had to change. I knew that Chloe liked being in the rocking chair, so I began getting her ready for bed, taking her into her darkened room and then feeding her in the rocking chair. As she fed, I would sing her a lullaby. When she was finished, I picked her up, tucked her into her cot, said goodnight and left the room. For the first few nights, she cried and cried as I left, so I began rocking her a little longer, until she was almost completely asleep, before putting her into her cot. Each night I did exactly the same thing and gradually I was able to put her into her cot sooner and sooner, now she can be quite awake when I leave her and she doesn't cry. Now it takes fifteen minutes to settle her when it used to take a few hours. I think Chloe feels safe and secure going to bed now because she knows what is coming next. She knows when we sit in the chair she'll get fed, she'll be sung a song and then she will be put in bed and then she goes to sleep. Looking back, I wish I had started a routine much earlier with Chloe and stuck to it, even if it meant a few tears. I think we would have both been a lot happier. When I think of all those hours I spent trying to settle her! Now bedtime is a relaxing end to the day for both of us.

Christina

Where should your baby sleep?

The question of whether or not to have your baby sleep in the same room as you, even in the same bed, or in a separate room, must be an individual, family decision and must take into account the needs of both baby and parents. There is no right or wrong decision, just what is right for your family. If both parents are good sleepers and like to have their baby close at night, then sleeping all together in a bed may be a time of loving closeness for everyone. If, however, one or both parents find it hard to sleep next to a tiny baby – which can happen for many reasons – then it may be better for the baby to be in a cot nearby, or even in a separate room.

'Babies can sleep anywhere'

Again, if you are reading this book before the birth of your baby, give yourself time to think and talk to your partner about all these possible night-time alternatives, then allow your instincts to guide you when the time comes. All parents are different, with their own habits, needs and circumstances. Your own instincts are the best. Your own experiments will show you the way. After all, parents were bringing up children long before there were childcare 'experts' and books!

Let's explore the possibilities:

Bed-sharing

Whether they had planned to or not, many parents find themselves sleeping in bed with their baby. Here are some of the benefits:

- The crying and screaming stop. A baby on his own at night may be roused to wakefulness not only by hunger – or perhaps a drop in temperature – but also by the release of stress hormones because his mother is missing.
- Lying down to breastfeed in bed is easy and peaceful for many mothers. The disruption of a night feed is often so slight that mother and baby barely wake up.
- Breastfeeding tends to continue for longer in bed-sharing families, which is a major benefit to mother and baby.
- Being in physical touch with his mother helps to regulate a baby's temperature, digestion, sleep cycle, heart rate and breathing, and his resistance to infection. Premature or ill babies need this continuous human contact most of all.
- Research by Dr. Michel Odent suggests that post-natal depression is less likely because the close bonding at night can speed up the rebalancing of a mother's hormone levels after birth.
- A working mother, away from her baby during the day, has more chance to bond with him and to grow close and confident. It makes up for lost hours together.
- A baby in bed with you gets touched and stroked more. Stroking a baby gives stimulus to his brain, which in turn encourages his healthy development. Some studies have shown that when babies are deprived of physical contact, they are more likely to grow into aggressive adults. (See Deborah Jackson's book *Three in a Bed*.)
- No more dragging yourself out of bed in the middle of the night!
- You have the comfort of knowing you will hear your baby's cry if he needs you.
- Your baby will not need to be moved after falling asleep in your arms or while feeding.

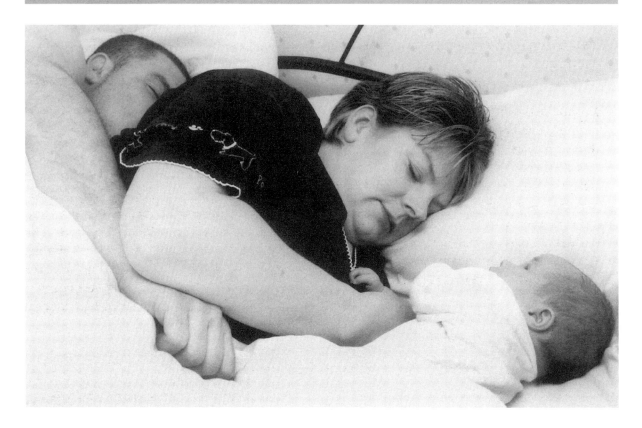

• My research suggests that a baby who has slept with, or close beside, a parent may have fewer nightmares later.

• In her book *The Continuum Concept*, Jean Liedloff suggests that the security of day-and-night contact in the earliest months helps a baby to grow naturally and rapidly towards trust and independence. She goes on to say that without sufficient physical closeness, babies can become stiffer, colder, more listless and less responsive in our arms. They may start to show little signs of frustration and petulance. Clinging, whining and tantrums may be more likely to start up later and they may make more demands on us rather than less as they become toddlers.

• FSID (The Foundation for the Study of Infant Death) recommends sleeping very close to your baby until the age of 6 months, as this has been found to reduce the risk of cot death.

In his book on 'Sudden Infant Death Syndrome', Dr James McKenna writes:

A baby's breathing rate slows down from about eighty-seven breaths a minute when she is new born to about forty-seven breaths a minute when she is a year old …

… This delicate change takes place mainly between two and four months and is considerably helped by sleeping close to a parent with the steadying effect of touch, warmth and a sense of an adult's slower breathing movement …

… Carbon dioxide breathed out by parents and breathed in, in small amounts, by a nearby sleeping baby acts as a chemical stimulant for her to take the next breath and so helps her find her own, slower rate, without difficulty or danger.

But be careful. There are some circumstances in which you should *not* have your baby in bed with you.

- Do not sleep with your baby if you or your partner have been drinking alcohol or taking drugs – *including over the counter medicines like cold remedies*. All these substances make you likely to sleep more deeply than usual. You may be less sensitive to your baby's presence.
- Do not sleep with your baby if you or your partner are ill or if you are very overtired.
- Do not sleep with your baby if you or your partner smoke. Lingering cigarette smoke on your skin, your hair and your breath can significantly increase the risk of cot death – Sudden Infant Death Syndrome or SIDS.

(Please see appendix at the end of this book for more information on cot death.)

Bed-sharing is becoming increasingly accepted. The Royal College of Midwives now explains and teaches bed-sharing 'good practice' to mothers, and UNICEF (United Nations Children's Fund) has developed a Baby Friendly Initiative for hospitals. This initiative encourages bed-sharing. Maternity nurses can then directly help mothers to know what to expect and how to cope with various night sleeping situations when they get home.

How to organize sleeping together

If you do decide to sleep with your baby, plan carefully. Below are some essential and useful details to consider.

Essential

A firm enough mattress to prevent him rolling into your 'valley' (no water beds).

- Make sure there are no gaps within or around the bed for the baby to slip into or where he might get wedged or squeezed. Check between mattress and wall, mattress and headboard, mattress and furniture, and between mattresses pushed together. An open rail headboard can be dangerous too – a baby might get his head caught in it.
- Keep him below or beyond the 'pillow line'. A baby cannot respond to a raised body temperature by pushing down the covers. His body temperature must be carefully regulated, taking into account the weight of the bedcovers and the body heat given off by his parents. If you plan to put your baby to sleep between you

both, use a lightweight separate cover for him – unless your own duvet is light enough. A thick adult duvet is too hot for a baby, especially when there is build-up of heat from his parents. The solutions are: to use a lighter duvet or fewer covers and to wear warmer nightclothes yourselves, or to dress your baby in only a cotton top and only a nappy below.

- Never sleep with your baby on a sofa. It's too squashy with no space to move or turn over.

Tips

- A roll of material under your baby's feet will help keep him in position if he starts to wriggle his way too far down in the bed.
- If you are worried about your baby falling out of bed, you might take the legs off the bed or put the mattress on the floor.

It can take about three weeks to settle down to the newness of having a tiny body in bed beside you and to learn to relax and sleep through the

We had Noah in the bed with us from day one, and I never had any worries about rolling on him. People would ask me, 'Well, what if you roll on him?' I just think naturally you don't. But I think bed-sharing did have something to do with my fears – because of things like cot death, I wanted him nearby, I wanted him right next to me, I wanted to hear him breathing. Our system was that he slept above our heads, with his own covers, so that we could never smother him, and it was fantastic. I was really sorry to give it up, but the reason I had to was that after eight months of sleeping all together, I wanted Hamish and me to have some time together. Then Noah went in his own bed in our room.

The only problem I had with it was if my husband, Hamish, was drunk, he had to sleep on the floor. 'He' meaning Hamish, not Noah! But it didn't happen very often and Hamish was fine about it.

We went to New Zealand for three months when Noah was four months old, and we hired a camper van and he slept between us there too … .

It was much easier for me to feed Noah in bed – I'd turn over, feed him, and I'd be less likely to wake up fully than if I got out of bed. I remember hearing women talking about getting out of bed and sitting in a chair, and I just can't imagine that. I get really cold and it is just much cosier to stay in bed.

I loved bed-sharing and I'll do it with the next baby, but probably not for as long. Noah would go to bed before us and then when we would get into bed and it was such a treat. We'd say, 'Shall we go to bed now? There's a little man waiting for us … ' And there he was, with his little squashed cheeks … lovely.

Caroline

little pantings and snufflings that start up occasionally. It's easiest of course if you never do anything else from the very beginning. After all, he's only moved a few inches away from where he has been for 9 months! Allow for the settling-in period with patience. Talk to your partner about any annoyances or difficulties that come up, and give each other extra loving attention.

In some cultures, having your baby in bed with you goes without saying. It's the normal way to live and to grow more instinctively sensitive and close to each other.

In some countries, children sleep close by a parent or grandparent until they are 6 or 7 years old and seem to develop a great sense of security and confidence by doing so. When a child has had enough experience of being in the arms of loving adults he will be less likely to become jealous of younger children and more likely to be happy to help care for them.

If you do have your baby in bed with you, by

In *The Continuum Concept*, Jean Liedloff says that:

When a baby has had all he needs of experience in his mother's arms and parts with her of his own free will, it makes him able to welcome with no difficulty the advent of a new baby in the place he has voluntarily left.

6–8 months he may be moving around much more during the night. He will already be better at controlling his own temperature and breathing and will probably have stopped having night feeds. You may decide that this is a good time to move him into a cot, close by at first maybe, then, when you think the time is right, into his own room. Some experts believe that making this first step towards a baby's independence at 6–8 months is worth a lot. Around 6 months is often a turning point for babies in all sorts of ways, and they don't mind or notice change as much at that age as when they are older. If you go on postponing the move into a separate bed you could find yourself a year later with a much

more alert and indignant toddler not wanting to leave your bed come hell or high water – and maybe another baby on the way.

No thanks!

Sleeping with a baby is not for everyone. For many good reasons, some mothers may not find it easy or practical to have their baby in bed with them:

- Some people feel very inhibited and unable to relax.
- One or both parents may be light sleepers – remember your baby needs you to be well rested.
- One partner would like to sleep with their baby but the other is not so sure.
- Having a baby in the bed may prevent you from making love.
- Some parents look forward to the night-time separation from their baby as a respite and time to recoup their energies.

- Older children may get furiously jealous and try to insist on joining in too.
- Though precautions can be taken to ensure the baby's safety while sleeping in a shared bed, some parents still feel too anxious to sleep well themselves.
- There may be social pressure to have your baby sleep in his own cot, or even in his own room.

> I don't want a wiggly baby in bed with me when I have been running around after it all day!'
>
> *Fran*

Halfway measures

Many parents don't feel quite right about having their baby in bed with them. At the same time, they may not want to put him in another room to sleep. There are several, excellent halfway measures.

Have the baby's cot in your room. Feed him in

your bed and return him to his cot afterwards.

Start with him in a cot when you settle him for the night but bring him into bed with you for his dawn feed (or feeds) and keep him there till morning.

Tie his cot firmly alongside your bed with its

'Both exhausted'

mattress built up to the same level as yours, or blocks put under the legs. Remove the side, so that he is sleeping in an extension of your bed. There are now specially designed cots for this purpose (see suppliers at the end of this book). Once he is weaned from night feeds, you can move the cot to another part of the room if that seems sensible. He will still sense your closeness even when asleep.

Put your mattress on the floor and an extra one alongside if you have room (big enough for him not to slip off, whatever wriggling he does).

Choosing for your baby to sleep in a separate room

You may choose to have your baby sleep in a separate, but nearby room. Perhaps you find it impossible to rest with a little one in the room. Perhaps you and your partner find you need time to be alone and intimate together without the baby right next to you. Perhaps one or both of you need your own sleeping space. Perhaps there are other reasons too. Sometimes it is hard for new parents to consider their own needs as well as their baby's. There is no right or wrong way, only what is best for your family. At the end of the day, your baby needs you to be as rested and happy as possible. That is the priority.

If you decide to have your baby sleep in a separate room, it helps if there is a connecting door to your room, or if the baby's room is very close by. Knowing you will easily be able to hear and respond if he needs you can be very comforting for you, and for him once he gets used to the arrangement and knows you are near. If the baby is unsettled at first, you may try having a grandparent, or even an older brother or sister, sleep on a mattress in the baby's room for a while. If you have other children, you may also think about having the baby sleep in the same room with them. A sleeping companion may mean longer and quieter sleeps, though older children can also be woken by babies, which would be hard on them!

We had always planned for Dylan to sleep in his own room, and the room was ready when he was born. At first he was in our room, but because our house is so small we actually had his cradle balanced on two chairs, which didn't feel that safe. So we knew he would go into his own room, we just never knew when. At six weeks he got a cold and he was snuffling all through the night, and every time he snuffled or breathed we woke up, so we were all exhausted. It then felt sensible to move him into his own room. We could hear what he was doing anyway because his room was so near – it's right next-door. Also, we had never intended to have him in the bed with us, and we didn't particularly want him in our room because we wanted time as a couple. We were a very short time together before I got pregnant, just a year, so we wanted to get to know each other after the baby was born without having him around. And the last reason was that I wasn't breastfeeding anymore at six weeks and so there was no practical reason to have him in our room.

Rhiannon

In a nutshell

Some of the key points we have covered in this chapter:

- A new baby will sleep for about 16 hours a day, gradually reducing to about 12 hours or so by around 6 months. There will be no settled pattern at first; these early months will be a gradual adjustment for the baby into a pattern of sleeping mostly at night and being awake mostly in the day.
- There are many ways we can try to soothe a baby to sleep; here are a few:

    - Allow him to suckle
    - Stroke his head, tummy or legs
    - Darken the room
    - Put a ticking clock near him
    - Swaddle or tuck him up well
    - Rock him
    - Walk around with him in your arms or in a sling
    - Sing to him or play soft, lilting music

- Find a solution that works for you and your baby and stick to it. The method will then become a 'sleep trigger' for your child. One person settling the baby at a time is a good idea, perhaps taking it in turns with your partner if you have one.
- Your new baby will be following his own sleep pattern at first. In these early days, he will wake in the night and expect to find you there. This can be an exhausting time for parents, so try to look after yourself and devise a coping strategy. Here are some tips:

    - Sleep when your baby sleeps or plan for catch-up sleep
    - Have everything you need for night feeds ready to hand
    - Make sure you are comfortable while breastfeeding, and in a safe position for the baby should you fall asleep
    - If you have someone to help you, consider taking it in turns to feed at night
    - If you are breastfeeding and need a good night's sleep, consider expressing some milk and allowing someone else to feed the baby

- Help your baby adjust to the pattern of day and night by establishing a bedtime routine.
- Where your baby sleeps is a family decision. Having your baby in bed with you is safe provided you take the precautions mentioned in this chapter; and if you choose not to, there are other options including having the baby's cot in your room or alongside your bed. Or you may find it hard to rest with a baby in the room and choose to have him sleep in another room nearby.

CHAPTER 2

Understanding a New Baby's Crying

It can seem that a new baby does nothing except feed, sleep and cry – not necessarily in that order. Anyone who has heard a baby cry knows that it is hard to ignore, and can be downright distressing. But often the distress for parents comes from not knowing what the baby needs or how they can help. This chapter will help you understand why your baby might be crying and offer you practical advice to help you respond with confidence. Be gentle with yourself. These early days are all about learning for your baby *and* you. It takes time and patience to understand your baby's needs, and occasionally earplugs!

Why do babies cry?

Crying is the only way your baby has to communicate with you. That is all it is – communication. When your baby cries, she is simply asking for her needs to be met in the only way she can. It may mean she is uncomfortable in some way, or it may just be that she wants to be close. If, when your baby cries, you can remember that it is just her way of talking to you and asking you for something, it will be easier for you to respond calmly and confidently.

Nature designed a baby's cry to be impossible for us to ignore, so that the baby grows and thrives. A baby's cry has to be loud enough to make sure we do not forget her for long, but help her at once when she is hungry, lonely or uncomfortable. And it needs to be piercing enough to jerk a mother out of sleep, and start breast milk flowing. It is a question of survival for babies. 'Is she good?' another mother may ask, meaning: Is she quiet? But ideas of good and bad cannot be applied to the way babies behave. Your new baby is not yet capable of doing something just to upset or to please you. She is not trying to manipulate you with her tears; she is just expressing a need. It is totally natural for babies to cry, and it is equally natural for you to find it upsetting.

Many parents will have found themselves at their baby's noisy cot-side at some deep hour of the night, their heart racing, their bodies having got there ahead of their minds. But some parents will find themselves waking up to such feelings of exhaustion and helplessness that they feel unable to move, despite the cries. They have been called back to their baby over and over again, night and day, racking their brains as to why she keeps crying so much and how ever to stop it.

Every baby is different

Each baby is born with her own, individual nature and therefore 'tastes', likes and dislikes. Some babies may not be bothered by noises, lights, feeling a bit hot or a bit cold, and the gurgles inside as their milk is digested, and will therefore be calm and sunny most of the time. Others will be disturbed by the slightest sensation and will call urgently for help and comfort in the only way they know. It's just the way they are made.

Different babies need different things. For example some babies are soothed by music or singing, other babies are stirred up by it and cry louder, as if it was a disturbance. Some babies need a lot of closeness and cuddling, others may need more space and quiet. Some prefer the room to be lighter or darker, quieter or with a buzz of background sound, wrapped up snug or with limbs free. It's also worth remembering that babies, like all of us, have different moods; and just because they were comfortable in one way yesterday doesn't mean that they feel the same today. When we recognise this, we can be more relaxed and flexible in our responses instead of becoming worried stiff every time the baby starts to cry.

Understanding your baby's cries

Knowing that every baby is different and has different needs, and that her needs may change, can leave parents feeling bewildered. But don't despair. Take a deep breath, watch, and think: What is going on? Some kind of change is needed. What could it be? Here's an example:

You have just fed, burped and changed your baby. You pass her to her father who has been looking forward to holding the baby all day. There is music playing in the sitting room and some friends have stopped by with their two children to say hello and catch a glimpse of the baby. For a while she seems peaceful, happy to be held and to gaze up at the different faces around her. Then suddenly she begins to cry. 'She was fine a minute ago,' someone says.

In this situation, the baby probably just needs a break from all the people and commotion; perhaps she needs just you for a while, or a little space and quiet. Maybe she is a baby that needs quite a bit of space and quiet, or maybe it just became too much for her at that moment, on

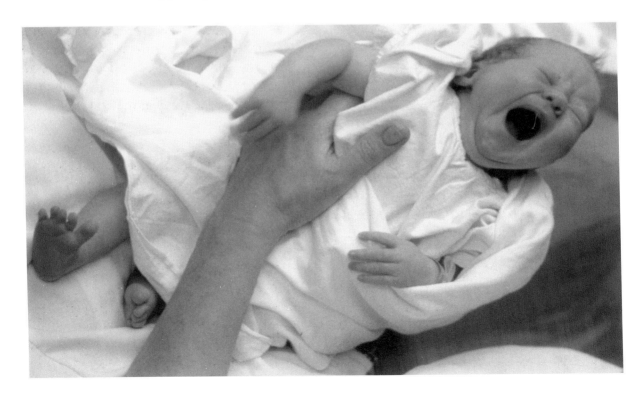

that day, and she'd be happy again after a little break from the noise. Only time, perseverance and experimenting will tell.

Listed below are some common causes of crying, and some suggestions for what you can do to help. One or another or several of them should work for you, especially if you persevere long enough for them to become familiar routines in the family. If you find that any of the suggested responses do not work or even stir your baby up, move on and try something else. You will learn valuable things about your baby and yourself. You will probably end up adding your own ideas to this list as well, and crossing others out, as you discover your baby's needs and what soothes her.

The 'Big Three' reasons babies cry

Because they are so aware of their baby's very basic needs, most parents are quick to check the big three possibilities:

- The baby is hungry.
- She is uncomfortable from trapped wind and needs to burp.
- Her nappy needs changing.

The baby is hungry …

The first possibility is that your baby is due for a feed and is hungry. If your baby is not due to feed, consider these other possibilities:

If you are breast-feeding …

The milk of breast-feeding mothers reflects their diet as well as their state of tiredness or well-being. Breast milk can become less rich and plentiful at the end of a busy day; therefore, babies who cry in the evening may just be crying from hunger because they have digested their last feed faster than usual. The baby will then want to feed more frequently to 'top up'. Frequent feeding also helps to stimulate the milk supply.

If your baby cries directly *after* a feed, she may be suffering from wind.

Some babies react badly to feeds after their mother has eaten things like curry, ginger or sudden large amounts of acid fruit – or has drunk stimulants like coffee, tea or cola. Very occasionally a baby is allergic to cow's milk protein and will be colicky after her mother has had milk or any other dairy products. For more details see section on colic in Chapter 3.

Things to try

- Rest in the afternoon and eat well.
- Breast-feed the baby more often in the evening if she is crying.
- If your baby suddenly cries more than usual, think – what did I eat today?

If you are bottle-feeding …

The quality of the feed is always the same but a baby who is very hungry or who is distressed because the milk is slightly too hot or too cold, may gulp at the teat and swallow air. If your baby cries after a feed, she may have wind.

Things to try

- Carefully check the temperature of the bottle.
- Burp the baby.

The baby needs burping …

Here is one simple burping technique:

- Hold the baby more or less upright, so the bubbles can rise. Make sure her chin is not right down on her chest, as that can block the passageway a bit.
- Slowly rub up and down her spine or give very, very gentle pats on her back.

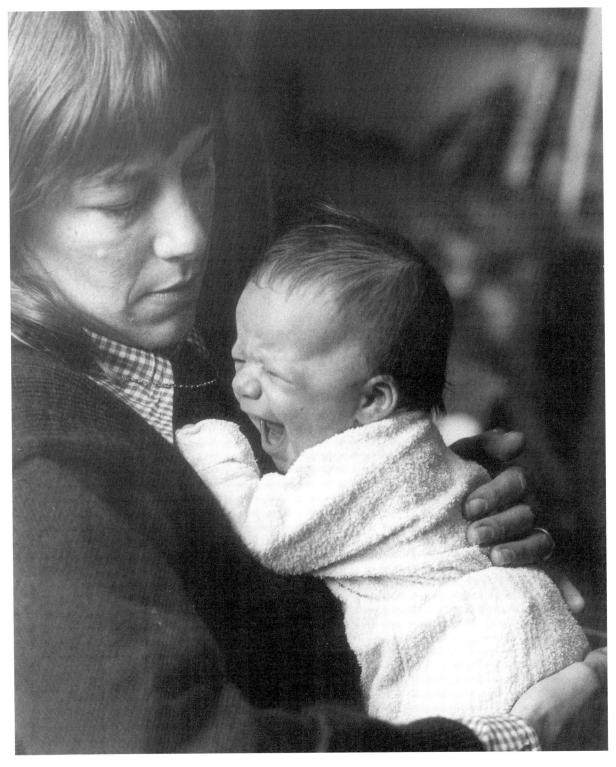

'Now, what kind of crying is that?'

Alternatively put her over your shoulder, with a cloth to catch any overflow, and walk about, or do the **Thumping Heel Sway,** described in the next section.

Burping usually works to release trapped air within half a minute.

The baby needs changing …

Babies vary enormously in their sensitivity to being wet. Some cannot bear a wet nappy, while others seem unaffected. Some will develop a rash at the slightest hint of wetness, and others do not. If your baby seems very sensitive to wetness, change her often, particularly if you are using washable nappies.

Most babies will not tolerate a dirty nappy. It is good practice to change nappies immediately they are dirty to prevent discomfort and skin irritation. A quick, close sniff will tell you.

Other possible reasons for the crying and how you can help

She is feeling lonely, cut off for too long from the sound of her mother's heartbeat and voice, her touch and her smell.

- *Gently stroke your baby or snuggle her against you, especially against your face, your neck and your chest. Try holding her in your arms longer and more often.*

Her eyes ache – Her eyes might need a rest from indoor lighting, or from sunlight. Also, research seems to be suggesting that babies need as complete darkness as possible at night to allow their sight to develop strongly and well.

- *Try turning the light off or closing the curtains.*
- *Make sure she is shaded while in the pram.*

She is too hot or too cold. Feeling her neck with two fingers will tell you whether she is chilly or sweaty.

- *Add or remove a layer of clothing.*

She is too tightly wrapped up
- *Loosen her blanket or sheet so she can stretch her arms and legs and get her fist to her mouth.*

Alternatively, she feels insecure and exposed. Maybe she would feel happier to be swaddled up.

- *Wrap her up securely like a little parcel, as she was in the womb (Please see Appendix A at the end of this book for more information on the benefits and risks of swaddling).*

Too much loud or continuous noise is hurting her ears. Loud or constant television, radio or shouting may cause her to cry at once in discomfort or take refuge in sleep to blot it out – then cry later to release the stress inside caused by the vibrations in her head.

- *Have some restful quiet time.*

She is over-stimulated. When awake, a baby is facing new experiences non-stop and needs to be allowed to practise focusing on objects and absorbing the changing sights and sounds from the safety of someone's arms. Too much talking, playing, tickling and efforts to get her to smile at us for too long at one time could well exhaust and tense her up and result in crying. Watch her eyes and expression carefully during 'play-time' and stop the stimulation as soon as there are signs that say 'Enough!'

- *Try giving your baby some space. Let her lie gently in your arms without any attention or put her down to sleep.*

Her head and neck are still uncomfortable and feeling the effects of her journey through the birth canal.

- *Allow the baby to suck as it triggers the release of special chemicals in her brain that reduce pain and stress.*

- **She is ill.**

- *Refer to the section entitled **Illness** in the next chapter for a simple 'look and listen' list of ways to tell if your baby is ill.*
- *With a young baby, it is always best to seek medical advice if you suspect she might be ill.*

Going outside

Sometimes just carrying a baby out of the door into the fresh air and daylight for a few moments is all that is needed to stop the crying. Sometimes walking a crying baby outside can relieve your tension too! This is a time when partners can most valuably take over and share in the care by providing a new pair of strong arms and legs, holding and walking their baby into calm or sleep. It's a fine way to draw closer together and develop a sense of belonging with each other.

Babies put to sleep outside in a pram are often quietened and fascinated by watching the shifting leaves on a tree if you can park the pram close to one. They also seem to sleep extra peacefully and deeply when they are outside. However you may encounter more traffic fumes and noise outside than fresh air and trees! If so, open a window wide on the quieter side of the building to have the sky almost overhead, and fresh air filling the room.

Carrying a crying or restless baby in a sling or pushing her in a buggy or pram usually puts her to sleep within a few minutes and is calming for both of you.

> **Precaution**   It's not sensible to leave a baby outside unattended with no one keeping an eye on her. Some mothers, for their own peace of mind, also like to use a pram net if there are cats or squirrels around.

Rhythmic movement

We humans love rhythm and movement! It seems to be something built in to us. While inside you, your baby experienced all your movements and was carried along in the rhythm of your walk. Moving rhythmically is the most natural thing for all of us, and can be a deep source of comfort for your baby. You may well find your tension slipping away as well. Rhythmic movement can be as simple as walking at a steady, rhythmic pace with your baby in your arms, or you can try swaying from side to side, or dancing together. If you need some help getting started, try The Thumping Heel Sway or The Swing and Dip Dance described on pages 34 and 35, and then expand to include your own movements as well. Your baby will love sharing movement with you, just as she did in the womb, no matter what steps you choose.

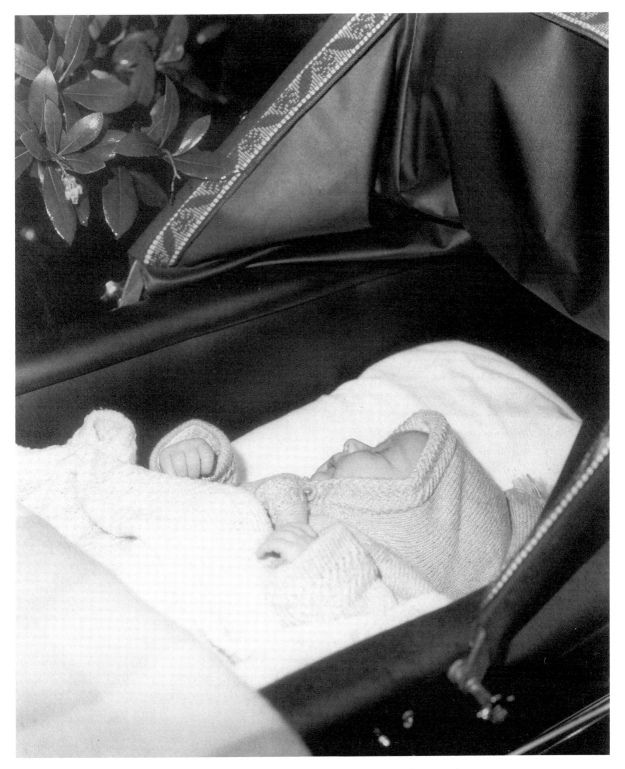

'Sleeping under the moving leaves of a tree'

The Thumping Heel Sway

Here is a simple and easy way to 'burp' a baby as well as to calm her if she starts to cry. It is a skill used by parents and carers all over the world:

1   Stand with your feet planted firmly and comfortably apart, just wider than your hips.

2   Hold your baby upright against your left shoulder at whatever level feels easy for you. If your shoulder is very bony or your baby is hiccoughy or sickuppy, lay a pad over your shoulder first. Left is best because she can feel your heartbeat more strongly that side.

3   Have one hand under her buttocks like an egg in an eggcup, and your other hand, with fingers spread, across her shoulders (or across her head and shoulders if she is still tiny and wobbly.)

4   Now, keeping the soles of your feet on the same spot, begin to sway your body slowly and rhythmically from left to right to left again, with stiff straight legs. Lift each heel in turn up off the ground enough to be able to thump it down again firmly with each body swing and send a heart-beat-like tremor up through your body into the child. This slow, steady thump … thump … thump of your heels bumping on the ground is mesmerising and comforting for both of you.

Because this is a graceful, rhythmic movement it is less tiring for you than walking anxiously up and down the room or sitting jiggling a baby, in all sorts of different positions, to try to stop the crying. Your own heartbeat and the extra 'heart-thump' of your heels on the floor have a doubly calming effect. Practise this until it becomes an easy and automatic movement.

When your baby is a little older, try holding her so that her head is pressed gently against your cheek and do some humming – mmm … mmm … – as you rock from heel to heel. Just two notes will do fine if you haven't a tune in your head at that moment. The sound vibrations fill her little body and may help to comfort her.

I used to bounce Ellie up and down on my lap when she cried and change her position in my arms all the time. The more she cried, the faster I jiggled her and the more often I turned her to face in another direction.

One day my auntie took her from me when she was screaming her head off. She just held her close over one shoulder and started a swaying movement as if she was beginning to dance in slow motion, with her heels clicking down on the kitchen floor. Ellie went quiet in half a minute. I couldn't believe it! Just watching them calmed me down too. I just stood there with a grin on my face feeling like an idiot. It's such an easy knack and hardly ever fails. I just never thought of it.

Veronica

The Swing and Dip Dance

If there are times when the Thumping Heel Sway fails to calm your baby, try this dance movement instead. It needs more daily practice and more energy but is usually well worth the extra effort. The Swing and Dip Dance comes from the work of nuns and parents training in baby and nursery care in Holland. It is based on a spiritual dance in India called Kirtan and versions of it are now practised in many different countries. It is one of the most loving and effective techniques taught for calming a distressed baby. When it works, it brings peace in a way that is wonderful to experience for the parent as well as for the baby. It lifts your baby down and up, as if from sky to earth and back again, like a game with gravity, and it swings her from side to side too. It gives her the same sensation she had in the womb when her mother was walking around and she, herself, was still small enough to swing and bob in the amniotic fluid 'like a ballet dancer in a swimming pool' as one gynaecologist described it, after watching ultrasound pictures of babies in the womb. Here are the step-by-step instructions:

1 Stand with your feet comfortably apart, holding your crying and probably struggling baby firmly but gently in your arms, across your chest with her head on whichever forearm feels most comfortable for you.

Try to gather your thoughts and be as calm as you can.

2 Stand still in this position for a few seconds, breathing quietly, listening with as much sympathy as you can to the noises of her crying, and feeling the jerking of her muscles against your arms and ribs.

Look into her face even if her eyes are closed up tight up with the crying.

3 Now, start the dance. Swing your weight across from your left foot onto your right foot. As you do so, lift your left foot off the ground and bring the tip of your big toe down beside your right foot.

4 As your left toe touches the floor, bend both your knees to make a little bob, like a curtsey, down and up again.

5 When you have straightened up, step and swing left with all your weight onto your left foot and bring your right foot to touch down, big toe first, alongside your left foot, bending your knees to make a second bob at the same time.

6 Keep going, stepping, swinging and bobbing from left to right again step ... bob ... up ... step ... bob ... up in a steady, rhythmic dance. *Watch her eyes all the time.*

There may be a good reason for the toe-tapping part of the dance. There are nerves all over our feet that connect directly to all the other parts of our body. The nerves at the top of our big toes connect directly to our brains. When the nerve endings in our big toes are stimulated by rubbing and pressure, they send a wake-up-and-do-your-best message in particular to the three small glands in the centre of our brains. These together act rather like the conductor of an orchestra bringing everything in the body into harmony through the hormones they secrete. When we have a baby in our arms who cannot easily be pacified, we need a bit of extra harmony and bodily ease ourselves to be able to cope.

7 If your baby is still crying loudly and desperately after two minutes, increase the depth of your bob and also swing the top half of your body around as you shift your weight from one foot to the other. Your baby will be making a curving movement in the air as well as swinging from side to side, and being dipped and lifted. Maintain a steady rhythm.

Keeping going is quite hard work at first until your knee and thigh muscles get stronger, which they will in a few days. If, at times, you feel too tired to lift your feet off the ground, don't worry, cut out the toe tapping and just swing your weight from one foot to the next without moving either, and let the dip slowly get smaller.

As soon as the swinging and dipping have become a steady automatic rhythm – so you don't have to think about it any more – see if you feel able to start humming or singing quietly at the same time, regardless of whether or not your baby is still crying. If you are feeling tired and silent, is there a possibility of playing a tape of gentle music? That can be comforting for both of you, and take the edge off the sound of the crying until it stops.

Now watch and see what happens

As this Swing and Dip Dance becomes familiar to your baby, after a week or so of practice it will comfort her more quickly. Each time you practise, keep an eye on the clock to see how long it takes before the crying begins to tail off and then stops (usually three or four minutes). After a week of practising, you will know whether this is something that helps like magic or isn't working at all. Just occasionally a baby needs stillness more than quick swinging movements, with continuous direction changes; this is particularly the case when a baby is in real physical discomfort or is ill.

When the Swing and Dip Dance does work, your baby will not usually fall asleep directly. She will suddenly relax in your arms and start gazing at your face, quite alert and happy. Keep swinging and dipping, but more slowly, maybe. She will then usually slip into a half-waking, half-dreaming state with flickering eyelids, half-shut eyes, shallow breathing and little, twitching half-smiling, half-sucking movements round her mouth. She is not really asleep yet. She is lost in her own enchantment of being alive and loved.

The next step is very important. Slowly stop the swinging and bobbing until you are standing still. Then either walk around or sit down quietly but keep holding her in your arms. Don't put her down until the flickering eyelid and shallow breathing state ends, and she either sinks into deep sleep with full breathing or opens her eyes wide, alert again and peaceful, ready to look around and enjoy life. Try not to break up the blissful, 'flickering' state by putting her down during it. This is likely to jerk her out of her bliss into feeling suddenly upset all over again – just what you want to avoid.

All you need do is to watch her face closely and listen to her breathing. Only when all the flickering and little twitches have stopped and her breathing has become deeper should she be put down somewhere, to free you for someone or something else.

It seems as if the combination of this particular swinging and dipping movement, along with being held against your heart, with eye contact – and maybe humming or singing as well – make up such a parcel of good things for a baby that a kind of wonder can envelop parent and child. If the Swing and Dip Dance does work for you and your baby, you will have developed a very special skill.

> I once stayed with a family in Holland. Their third son, 2 months old, had had a difficult birth, and you could see he was still 'wound up' because he did a lot of twisting about and crying, even when he was being held. Comforting him seemed almost impossible. His mother began to use the 'Swing and Dip Dance', which she had learnt from the nuns running the Sunrise Nursery where she had worked. It didn't make much difference at first, then suddenly, after about a week, the movements became really familiar to him and started to have a wonderful effect. He would stop crying almost immediately. It was as if he was able to relax at last.

Wheels

You may sometimes find yourself too tired to hold your crying baby in your arms any longer or you may need a free hand to do something else. Or your baby may simply be getting more distressed and wound up the more you hold her. Sometimes babies get over-stimulated by being held, usually because, like a sponge, they absorb some of your anxiety as you try to rock or jiggle them in your arms to quieten them. And sometimes you just need to be at arms' length from the crying spasms!

If this is the case, however loudly she is crying, wrap her snugly and lay her down in the familiar nest of a pram or buggy. Find enough space wherever you are to push it at arms' length. Stand or sit down comfortably. You may have to push and pull for quite a while, because, if you stop before she is completely calm, she may redouble her crying, in protest.

If wheeling on its own fails to do the trick, try this: put a ruler or a cloth folded into a narrow strip on the floor for one of the back wheels to run over every time you push and pull. The little wobbly jolting it makes will often send a baby quickly to sleep, when all else has failed.

There may be times when all of your efforts to soothe your crying baby fail. The crying may get worse and worse until it sounds more like screaming, and it is then time to look for a deeper cause for the distress. We'll look at this in the next chapter.

'Going outside'

In a nutshell

- It is totally natural for your baby to cry. It is her way of communicating with you. She is simply telling you that something in her environment needs to change.
- It is totally natural for you to find the sound of your baby's cries upsetting. Nature designed it that way so that the baby's needs would be met.
- Every baby is different. Some like to be soothed in one way; some in another. It is a matter of finding out what works for you and your baby. Experiment and see.
- A baby's needs can change over time and in different circumstances, so try to be flexible.
- There are lots of different messages your baby may be trying to give you by crying, and there are lots of things you can do to soothe her.
- The Big Three causes of crying:
  - Your baby is hungry
  - Your baby needs burping
  - Your baby needs changing

Other possible causes of crying

Cause	What to do to help
She is lonely	*Hold her longer and more often*
Her eyes ache	*Turn off lights*
	Close curtains
	Shade the pram
She is too hot or too cold	*Add or remove a layer*
She is too tightly swaddled up	*Give her legs and arms room to move*
She feels insecure and exposed	*Wrap her securely*
Her ears hurt	*Have some restful, quiet time*
She is over-stimulated	*Give her some space and quiet*
She is hungry for touch and smell	*Stroke, cuddle and snuggle her*
She has birth pain in her head and neck	*Allow the baby to suck to release pain-reducing chemicals in the brain*

- Going outside if you have a balcony, garden or yard can be very soothing for your baby and for you. Enjoying nature together can relieve stress and draw you closer as a family.
- Babies are soothed by fresh air and often sleep more peacefully outside or by an open window … with an adult close by.
- Babies love rhythmic movement. It is a good stress-reliever for you too. Rhythmic movement can be as simple as walking at a steady, rhythmic pace with your baby in your arms, or you can try swaying from side to side, or dancing together. If you need some help getting started, try The Thumping Heel Sway or The Swing and Dip Dance described in detail in the chapter.
- The movement of wheels can often soothe a baby. This is particularly helpful if you are feeling too tired to carry your baby around.

CHAPTER 3

When Crying Becomes Screaming

Screaming is crying that has gone into the next stage. Here are some ways to recognize the difference:

- Screaming is a panicky sound
- Screaming intensifies as it goes on
- Screaming may start off at an alarming pitch, or may begin as crying, grow into more determined crying, then turn into screaming
- Some babies have a regular time for screaming, like the early evening.

A young baby who is distressed has no means of comforting himself. He relies on his parents to do it for him. At this very young age he is unlikely to 'cry himself out'. On the contrary, the anguish of a baby left alone builds up rapidly. Because he has no sense of time, he cannot wait with any expectation that his parent will return to rescue him. The feeling that help will never come overwhelms him. He feels alone and frantic with fear and loneliness.

Of course there are times when the baby must be left for a few minutes while you look after other children or if you are in the middle of a task you can't abandon instantly. But in these early days it is best to attend to him as quickly as possible. 'Now' is still the only sense of reality he has. Once he is several months old he will have lived long enough to experience and remember that you always do come back to him when he needs you, and that panic or pain do always come to an end.

Physical causes

Colic, dirty nappy and soreness are the most common physical causes of screaming. Check them all. Don't assume that because one thing made the baby scream the last two times, it will necessarily be the same again. However, your baby may have tendencies towards certain things like nappy rash or colic; if so, consider those possibilities first.

Colic

Colic is the word we use to describe an acute, digestive spasm, which hurts in waves and makes a baby writhe, draw his knees up over his tummy, tense and jerk, and scream in distress or rage. Though wind is a normal part of the digestion, the discomfort of what is happening inside makes the task of comforting and silencing the baby particularly difficult.

- **Colic is often due to the immaturity of the baby's bowel.** This will right itself as the baby grows and develops.
- **Colic is sometimes caused by gulping in too much air with the milk**. Some babies, as they grow stronger and hungrier during the first weeks, suck so fast and furiously at the start of a feed that this air-intake is difficult to avoid. Here are some suggestions that may help if your baby is swallowing air:

  - If you are bottlefeeding, make sure you tip the bottle steeply enough to keep the air inside it away from the baby's mouth, and remove the teat every now and then so a vacuum does not build up in the bottle to make the baby suck furiously and so swallow air.
  - If you are breastfeeding, make sure that the whole of your nipple is far enough into the back of his mouth. Ask your midwife or health visitor to help you if necessary.
  - Try starting a feed *before* the baby has begun to cry with hunger.

- **If you are breastfeeding, colic can be caused by something you have eaten.** Elements of the foods you eat reach your baby through your milk. Some babies react badly to elements in certain foods. For example, occasionally babies get severe colicky pains and scream because they find it difficult to digest the cows' milk protein that passes directly to them through their mother's milk. If you suspect this is the case it might be worth cutting out cows' milk, butter, cream, cheese and margarines, that include whey, from your

own diet for a few days to see if there is an improvement. But talk to your health visitor or doctor first to make sure you know how to replace the calcium, proteins and vitamins you need in your diet. Other foods that commonly cause colicky pains include curry, ginger, sudden large amounts of acid fruit, and drinks that contain stimulants like coffee, tea or cola. If you think your baby may be suffering from food-related colic, try to identify and limit 'problem' foods in your diet.

Here are some other suggestions if you think your baby is suffering from colic:

- Your baby's colic may be caused by his inability to digest the lactose in his milk. If so, a drop or two of a remedy called 'Colief' will work wonders. (See Suppliers List at the end of this book). Drinking fennel tea yourself may also help him.
- Unless there is a medical reason to do so, try not to feed more often than two-hourly and give a sip or two of cold water a short while before, to bring up any wind.
- Lie the baby face down, along one arm with his head near the crook of your elbow so that the 'heel' of your hand is pressed up against his tummy. Lay your

'Redundant cow'

other arm alongside him, your hand spread around his ribs. Walk about like this or rock gently. You may not know whether this helps until you have tried it several times over a week, and the position has become familiar to him.

- Try flexing the baby's knees gently towards his chest.
- There are baby massage techniques to ease colic. Ask your health visitor or find a good book on the subject. See *Useful Books* list at the end of this book.

Nappy needs changing

Leaving the nappy off for a while may help. Being able to kick freely can help to get rid of the stress.

Sore bottom

This may be the cause of the screams, whether or not the nappy needs changing. Washing with plenty of water, drying carefully and leaving the nappy off for a while to let air and maybe sunshine reach the skin for a few minutes will help. If you are using washable nappies, apply cream to protect from the next wetting. Cream can interfere with the absorbency of disposable nappies and so leave the baby wetter than without cream. It is OK however if only a very little cream is used and it is well rubbed in.

Hunger pangs and thirst

This can drive some babies to the screaming stage too. And screaming itself can dehydrate a baby quite quickly.

Illness

A baby may well scream and cry when he feels ill, or go floppy and unresponsive. It is always best to seek medical advice if you feel your young baby is unwell and you are unsure of the cause.

When a baby is crying, parents urgently want to know what the signs are which will tell them that their baby is unwell. If this is their first baby, it can be especially difficult to judge whether or not illness is the cause of the crying.

The easiest look-and-listen checks are these:

- Is it an unusual cry – more high-pitched, frail or moaning than normal?
- Has your baby sicked-up most of his last feed(s)?
- Are his eyes withdrawn, not watching you and not looking out at anything, even when he is not actually crying?
- Is he drawing in his breath in a tense or wheezy way – even when he is not crying – instead of breathing easily as babies should?
- Has he got a rash – over quite a big area of skin?
- Has he got a temperature?

It is important to note that perfectly healthy babies can exhibit any of these symptoms as well, but if you sense he is unwell it is best to seek medical advice. For more information on diagnosing illness, you might like to buy a small booklet called *Babycheck, Is Your Baby Really ILL*. *Babycheck* has been scientifically developed by a team of paediatricians based in Cambridge. It describes nineteen simple checks for different signs of illness in a baby and helps you decide, through a scoring system, whether or not your baby needs to be seen by a doctor. Find details in the Useful Books list at the end of this book.

Birth trauma and cranial osteopathy

Another cause of screaming in the early weeks could be birth trauma. Birth can be one of the most physically traumatic events of our lives.

Huge forces during birth cause a baby to twist and turn as it travels through the bony pelvis and down the birth passage. In all normal

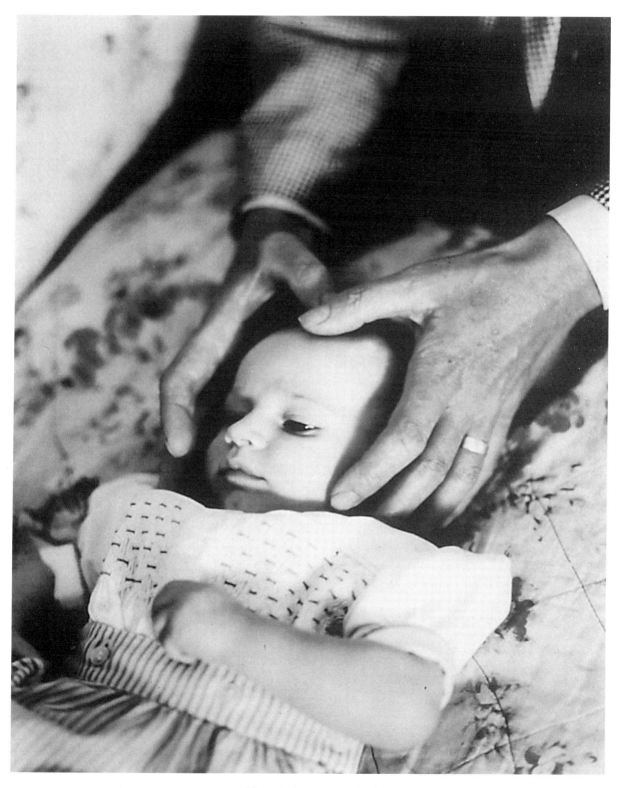

'Cranial osteopathy'

deliveries, the baby's head takes the strain and is moulded and shaped by the pressures of birth – this protects the baby's brain. A newborn baby's head is made up of membranes, cartilage and areas of growing bone which are still pliable and are able to bend, shift and even overlap to make the birth journey possible through such a narrow pathway. In the first few days, as the baby suckles, yawns and cries, the forced moulding of the head gently rights itself.

Cranial osteopathy is a specialist technique that has been found to give valuable help to newborn babies and young children who are unsettled and difficult for no apparent reason, during the first weeks, months or years of their lives. The thinking behind it is that sometimes the head does not have enough elasticity to recover its right shape after birth and there are hidden stresses left behind for the baby to bear as best he can. When this is so, the delicate balance between the structures forming the baby's head and the central nervous system is upset, causing discomfort. This can result in many different problems such as crying, fretfulness, breath holding, colic and sucking problems in tiny babies. Later on it can show in skin problems, hyperactivity, bed-wetting, tummy aches, head-aches and all sorts of nervous upsets in older children.

Babies who may be helped by cranial osteopathy are those who

- have had a difficult birth, perhaps being delivered finally by forceps
- have had births which have been too quick, not allowing sufficient time for moulding to take place
- have had a caesarean delivery
- suffer from colic, sickness and wind or have feeding difficulties

> Our son and his wife had twins last year, both fine, strong babies, but one of them had difficulty breathing and was in intensive care for a few days. When they came home from hospital a week later, he was still restless and he cried a lot. A Cranial Osteopath treated him twice, only for ten or fifteen minutes each time. He relaxed at once under her fingertip touch and just gazed at her, then slept deeply for hours. The change was instant and wonderful to watch. The tension in him just seemed to fly out of the window.
>
> *Steve*

- are very withdrawn; who seem to sleep all the time, never crying or moving much
- can't sleep for any length of time
- fail to thrive
- also older babies who headbutt or headbang.

The therapist applies very gentle pressure around the head, neck and spine, barely more than a steady touch on exactly the right spots. This can help the baby's natural self-healing processes to start working properly again so that the stresses that have been left behind and become 'a habit' since birth, are finally released.

Cranial osteopathy treatment is very gentle, safe and effective for babies and children. It works fastest and best of all for children under five but can help people at later stages of life if help is still needed.

Cranial osteopathy is carried out by trained practitioners. There are addresses and details for you about cranial osteopathy in the resources list at the end of this book.

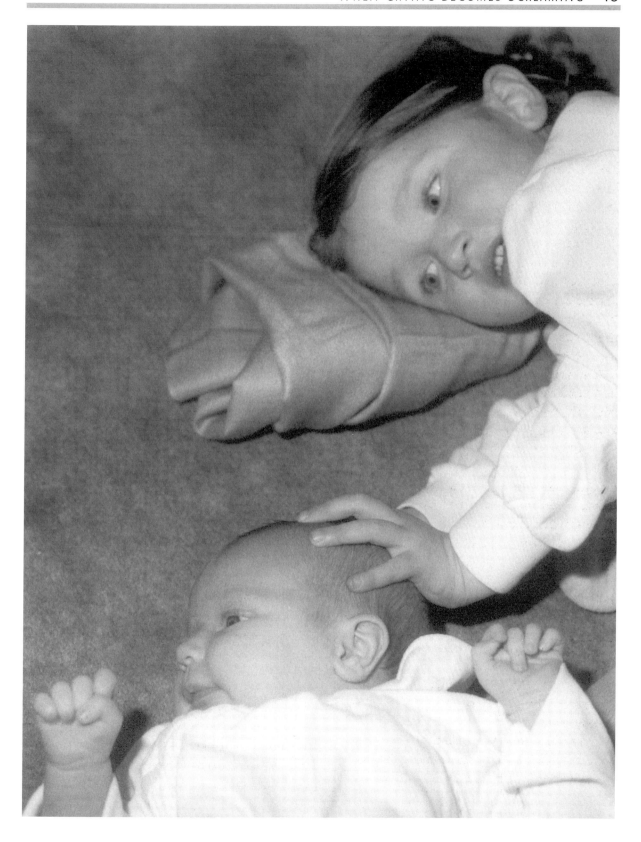

Emotional causes

Even if you have found a physical cause for the screaming and put it right, your baby's distress may continue to mount. Or you may have checked everything you can think of and can't find anything immediately wrong – he just seems to be desperate and desolate. This can be confusing and exhausting for parents.

It isn't always the parent's job to stop the screaming as soon as possible. Your baby may *need* to scream. Screaming *can* be a *good* thing. Babies have an emotional life as well as a physical one. They undergo stresses just like adults do; only sometimes their reactions can be all the stronger because they can't talk and tell you what they are feeling. Releasing now, through screaming, whatever tension the baby is holding, may prevent the misery becoming bottled up and flaring up later in childhood as grief and tantrums.

It is important to remember that crying and screaming needn't be anyone's fault, and needn't have a physical cause that you can do anything about. A baby can become panic-stricken by his own reactions. He may begin to cry or scream because of a physical pain of some kind, then the crying and screaming quickly escalates as he frightens himself with the sound of his own screaming. It becomes a spiral of distress. Some babies who keep crying for hours, despite all our care, may be suffering from 'prenatal trauma' or 'birth trauma'. It is worth considering these causes.

My baby never stops crying – I just feel sick and exhausted all the time.
Fintje

What can we be doing wrong?
Steven

It makes you feel a failure – it's as if it's your own fault somehow.
Annice

Please help me before I do something terrible!
Roberta

For four months, it was like having a relative come to stay who hated us!
Fernando

I once watched a wonderful dad bring complete peace to his screaming baby in just a few minutes through his own matter-of-fact acceptance and love for his child. This is what he did: He lolled right back in an armchair so his chest was just a gentle slope. Then he laid his baby, screams and all, on his front on his chest, so that the baby's heart and his heart were 'in touch'. The baby had his head turned sideways just under his dad's chin and was crying with every breath. Dad's hand was cupped under his bottom so he could not slip down or sideways. Dad kept absolutely still and just let the baby carry on crying without fuss or interference. All the time he just went on talking to us, two visiting friends, as if nothing was wrong or awkward. In what seemed no time at all the crying stopped and the baby slipped into a calm and blissful sleep. The conversation just carried on. We couldn't take our eyes off the two of them.
Maggie

of her baby's development in the womb, her baby can become affected by her sadness or fright. An unborn baby can also pick up feelings by listening to his parents' voices – their kind tones, their happy chattering and singing or their angry shouting. His crying now helps to release the tension that built up in him then. He can't look back and talk his way through the sadness or worry as his mother can, so he just bawls his head off until the tension begins to fade away and life gets rosy again. There are all sorts of ways to help this happen for him. (See the 'How to help' section which follows.)

Birth trauma

Earlier in the chapter we discussed the physical effects of birth trauma, but there can be emotional ones as well. Mothers giving birth know what is happening and they have people around to encourage and comfort and help them through it. The baby is alone, suddenly experiencing a long, frightening, exhausting, usually painful time. If it has been a prolonged or a hard birth, if there were complications, or the hands receiving the baby were rough and hurried, the noises loud, the light painfully bright, the baby will have suffered extreme strain and stress.

If a mother guesses that her baby is likely to be carrying some degree of after-shock from the birth, it is easier to accept, without too much anxiety, the crying that may follow for the first few weeks or months. The stress has got to be released bit by bit.

Prenatal trauma

The term 'prenatal trauma' refers to feelings of anxiety and distress experienced by the baby before birth. This can happen because babies, even before they are born, are very sensitive to their mother's emotions, as the chemicals from the activity of her brain feed into them through the umbilical cord. If, for example, something really sad or horrible happens to a pregnant mother, particularly during the last few months

Bearing the anguish

Coping with a young baby who seems to cry and scream for hours every day can be devastating for parents. Not knowing the cause of the distress or how to help can leave you feeling confused and powerless.

Try to remember that this is a phase; it won't last forever. The question is how to best support your baby and yourself through this challenging time.

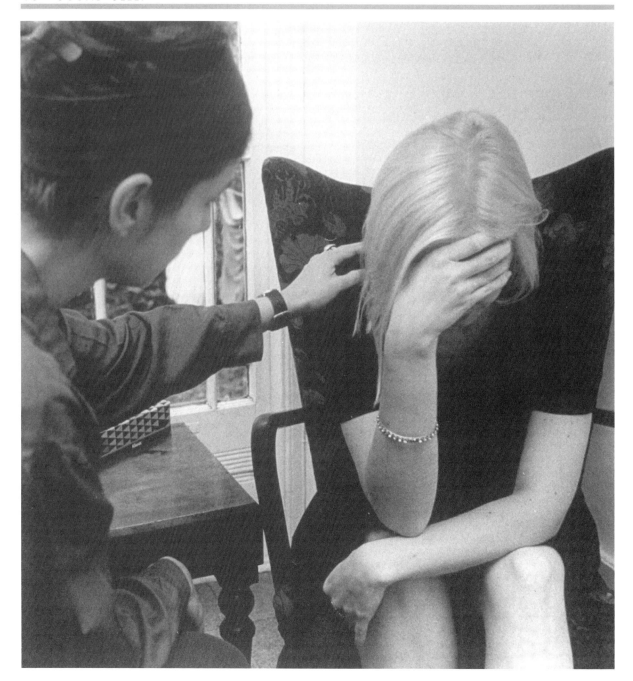

How to help

Once you have checked the baby for physical discomforts, sometimes you can only guess what is the main cause of all the crying. In a way, it doesn't matter whether you know or not, because the same responses are needed for any unhappy baby, whatever the cause.

Most of all, he needs to be in someone's accepting and loving arms – someone wearing ear plugs if necessary! – so that his tension can begin to drain away through their body. He needs your understanding that he is helpless and needs to be held, maybe even for many hours, over the next few weeks. His skin needs to be touched, stroked and, if possible, his whole body gently massaged as a regular habit. Just with fingertips only, if he is still only a few weeks old. Ask your midwife or doctor about this massage.

In Chapter 2 we looked at lots of loving ways to soothe your crying baby. These same methods can be used to soothe a screaming baby and can even act as healers of past traumas. Things that remind him of the womb may be particularly useful; such as, rhythmic sound or music with a beat in it, like a heart-beat, or swinging and rocking movements.

- Try the rhythmic movements of the Thumping Heel Sway and/or the Swing and Dip Dance described in Chapter 2.
- Use distraction techniques such as showing your baby something interesting to look at, perhaps some flowers or the wind blowing the leaves on a tree. Take him into a different room or outside. Sing or hum your favourite tune to him.
- If it is possible, you could try getting into a warm bath together.

If you have help within reach, try giving the baby to another person for a while. A new pair of arms, a different smell and voice, may break through the spiral of distress. And it will give you a break.

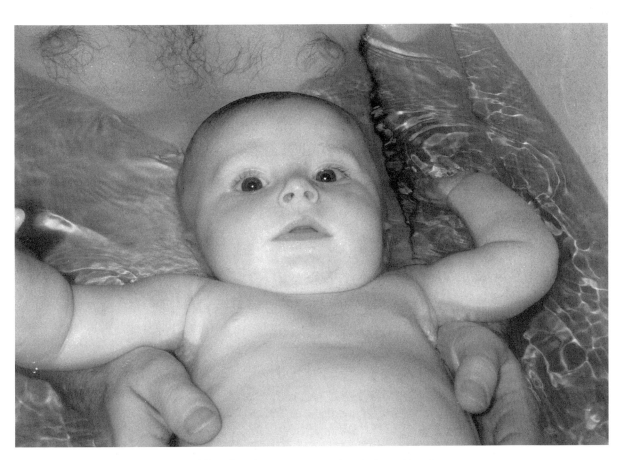

'Getting into a warm bath together'

Helping yourself

When we first hear our baby scream, it is instinctive to pick him up and hold him close. But when you hold and touch a screaming baby to bring comfort, it is harder altogether because it becomes necessary to calm yourself at the same time. Your heart is probably already racing in response to the screams; you need to get rid of your own panicky feelings before they transmit themselves to your baby. Try humming or putting on music that soothes you. Take the baby to a part of the room that pleases you, to a picture or something else that you love to look at, or walk with him to look out of the window. This will take your mind off the baby's distress just enough to allow you a little distance.

If all else fails and you are starting to feel really stressed – even scared of what you might do in your anger and despair – put him down in his cot or basket or carry cot and leave the room for ten minutes. Give yourself a breathing space before you return. The general rule of never leaving a young baby to scream needs to be broken when you are feeling desperate. Find someone to talk to if you can. Failing that, give yourself a moment and look at the next chapter, *How to Cope with Crying and Screaming.*

Remember, this <u>is</u> a temporary state of affairs and you do not have to carry on doing everything as usual. Try to think of changes you could make in your life to support yourself and your baby. Here are a few suggestions:

- Call in help whenever you can find it – from friends, family and trusted neighbours.
- Talk to your doctor, midwife or other medical staff.
- Talk to other parents of young children. Many people will know what you are going through. Sharing the worry and frustration really does help.
- Look at your diet. If you are breastfeeding, are you eating anything that might be upsetting your baby? Whatever feeding method you use, are you eating well enough to sustain yourself?
- Is there anyone you could ask to help with arrangements like picking older children up from school?
- Are there any favours you are doing for anyone else which could be temporarily shelved?
- Are there any changes you could make to your living and sleeping arrangements to help you go with the flow more? You must catch up on lost sleep somehow! Notice if there is a time of day when your baby does usually sleep uninterruptedly for several hours. Grab the chance and dive back into bed or relax in a chair – even if it is just after breakfast and even if your mind is full of jobs needing to be done. Tip guilt out of the window, ignore convention. You will be able to do those jobs much faster and more cheerfully later. Put a 'Please don't disturb' notice on the door, turn the ringer off on the telephone, and lend your toddler, if you have one, to someone else for two hours.

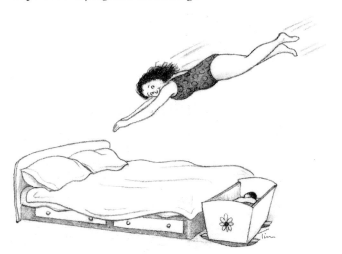

'Diving back into bed'

In a nutshell

- Screaming is crying that has gone into the next stage.
- Screaming may start off at an alarming pitch, or may begin as crying, grow into more determined crying, then turn into screaming.
- Some babies have a regular time for screaming, like the early evening
- The only reality for a young baby is 'now'. They have no sense of time. A young baby is unlikely to 'cry himself out'. It is best to attend to a young baby that is crying or screaming as soon as possible.
- Once the baby is several months old, he will begin to understand that you always do come back and you are there when he needs you.

- **Physical causes of screaming include**
  - Nappy needs changing
  - Soreness in the nappy area
  - Colic
  - Hunger pangs or thirst
  - Illness
  - Birth trauma

- **Emotional causes of screaming include**
  - Prenatal trauma
  - Birth trauma
  - Babies can frighten themselves with the sound of their own crying and screaming
  - Screaming can be a good thing. It is a way of releasing tension and stress the baby is holding.

- Most of all, a screaming baby needs to be in someone's accepting and loving arms so that the tension can begin to drain away through the other's body.
- Refer to Chapter 2 for ways to soothe your baby, particularly using rhythmic movement and sound.
- Use distraction techniques such as showing him something interesting, taking him outside, or singing a favourite tune.
- If it is possible, you could try getting into a warm bath together.
- Try giving the baby to another person for a while. A new pair of arms, a different smell and voice, may break through the spiral of distress. And it will give you a break too.

CHAPTER 4

How to Cope with Crying and Screaming

Sometimes I feel so angry with him, I end up throwing him onto the bed and shouting at him.

Claire

How can you comfort a baby when she won't even suck? I get so upset I want to give up and walk out of the house.

Milly

Some days I just want to shake him and shake him to shut him up.

Emma

Feeling hate for your own baby is like being in hell. You can't tell anyone what you are feeling when it's as bad as that.

Esther

One day I'm going to end up hitting her when I can't stand the noise one more minute.

Ruth

Most parents in the world, especially new mothers, are likely to feel a few such moments of bleak misery at one time or another. When your baby cries and screams often enough and for long enough to upset you that badly, you may feel frustration, anxiety, panic, rage, guilt, even hatred. You may have a sense of failure, of hopelessness, of being trapped, of disliking your child and fear that you'll never be able to cope, or that you might hurt her. You may find it hard to believe that things will get better. You may feel too frantic to think clearly.

Link with your own babyhood

The anxiety we feel at these times may link directly back to our own babyhood and childhood experiences. When we become parents, some of our reactions are likely to be influenced by what happened to us all those years ago. There may have been painful and difficult experiences in our own babyhood and young childhood, which are now echoed in the sounds of our own babies' crying. If you think that memories or feelings from your childhood could still be hurting you, try to find someone to talk to as soon as you can. (See Help, Support and Useful Addresses section at the end of the book.)

Other troubles now?

How are you? Is there a big worry in your life just now? If so, try to do something about it. Is that possible? Talk. Be honest. Ask for help. Babies and young children are very sensitive to their parents' moods. If you are depressed and anxious, your behaviour changes in many subtle ways. Your child will reflect your stress like a little mirror and her crying in turn may be the last straw to add to your own burden of worry. Mothers on their own without a partner there to share, talk, support and make light of hard times, are doubly alone. Until you feel better yourself it will be hard to concentrate on soothing and helping your baby. (Please see Appendix C at the end of this book for more information on Post-natal Depression).

Feeling lonely and isolated

Many parents of young babies suddenly feel very alone and cut off, once the excitement of the birth has died down. Motherhood can even begin to feel like imprisonment, especially if you don't feel ready yet for walking far or going visiting. The rest of the world can seem to be flowing on around you while you have been left stranded, just you and your baby and the incessant crying. Self-doubt, self-blame and churning emotions towards your baby are not unusual. You may feel you want to hide these feelings away. But remember, other people are going through the same thing. Talking to people can really help.

See if there are groups and activities for mothers and babies in your area. If your circumstances make it impossible to get out to meet people, invite a friend to visit you. This can mean practical help with the baby as well as company for you.

The need to stand back

Sometimes we may find ourselves wishing that parenthood had not enveloped us so completely and utterly. Occasionally it's possible to forget for a moment that it has! However, the reality of a crying baby soon brings us back to earth and the need to think things through, make decisions and take action. To be able to do this, you need to stand back emotionally somehow, and think long term as well as short term. Some of the following ideas may help you to do this.

Looking after yourself

How many mothers, particularly new mothers, have days when at four o'clock in the afternoon they've not yet brushed their teeth, their hair, or perhaps even got dressed! It is so easy to focus on the often overwhelming needs of a tiny baby and completely forget about ourselves. But our babies need us to feel as relaxed and as happy as possible, and it is much easier to feel rested and calm if we look after ourselves.

Think of things you enjoy doing, things that make you feel relaxed and good about yourself . Try to find time to do them, even if it's for just a few minutes at a time. The possibilities are endless, but here are a few suggestions to get you thinking:

- Talk to friends
- Read a book, newspaper or magazine
- Exercise
- Cook something you like to eat
- Watch T.V. or a video you've looked forward to
- Lie on the grass under a tree – or go to a beautiful place just to look around and feel peaceful
- Soak in a warm bath
- Have a massage; this does not have to be a professional one: a friend or partner can do it for you
- Stroke your cat, dog or rabbit!

Looking after yourself also means keeping an eye on the way you try to organize your day. Babies find peace from the calm we give them. Continual hurrying and worrying can only make you both feel worse. Which things could wait a day, a week or a month? It's more important now to rest whenever you can and to eat well, particularly if you are breastfeeding.

Ask for help and support

Turn to friends, family and neighbours with experience and ask for their advice, or just their sympathy. Don't be afraid to ask the professionals. Health visitors in particular are very used to helping parents under stress. Your doctor or other medical staff will also be able to offer support and practical advice.

Parentline and CRY-SIS provide telephone helplines for parents with distressed and crying babies and toddlers (addresses and telephone numbers in the National and voluntary organisations and helplines list at the end of this book).

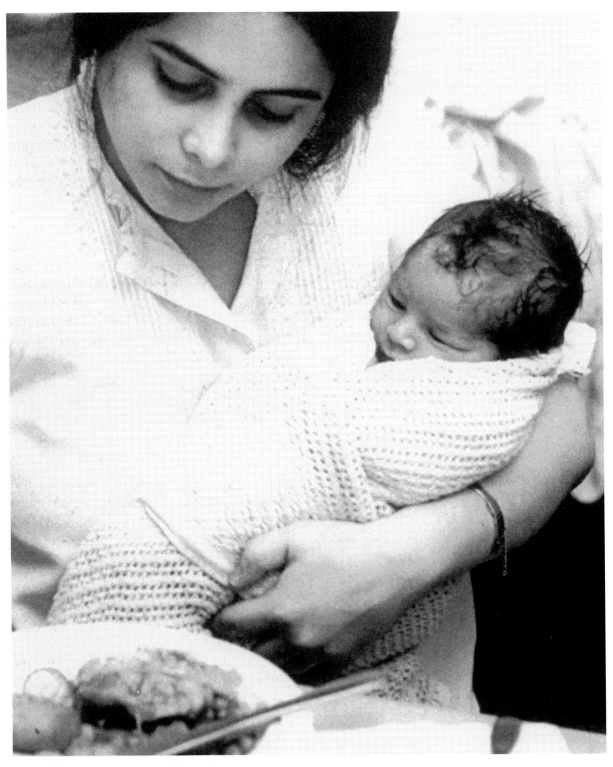

'Rest whenever you can and eat well'

Try making a 'Crying Diary'

The next practical and valuable step you may want to take is to make a 'Crying Diary' – accurate details of *when* your baby cries or screams, *for how long* each time and *what you do about it* each time it happens. Keep this 'Crying Diary' for a week, writing everything down as it happens. Don't bother to include little 3- or 4-minute crying spells.

Making a 'Crying Diary' helps in two different ways:

- It gives you more confidence because you are doing something about the problem. You can listen to the crying with a more detached ear – not just the ear of a miserable, worn-out parent.
- It provides you with an accurate picture. Exhaustion makes it hard to remember exactly what happened and when, or to judge what our reactions were, a day or two later. Things that distress us become confused or exaggerated in our minds unless we write the details down at once. Now you can see how much your baby really is crying during 24 hours. You can see what has calmed her, and what has not, and can start to think about, and try out, other methods suggested in this book and see which begin to work.

On the following page is one example of a Crying Diary, but make one for yourself any way you like.

If your life is like a madhouse with several older children to look after as well as a little screamer, you may decide that keeping a careful diary would be an impossibility. However, even a quick scribble on the shopping list or on a calender can add up to a good enough record to help you.

In a nutshell

- Coping with a crying or screaming baby is very stressful and can bring up powerful emotions for even the most patient of parents. When your baby cries and screams often enough and for long enough, you may experience any or all of the following:

  - Frustration
  - Anxiety
  - Panic
  - Rage
  - Guilt
  - Hatred
  - Confusion

You may feel
  - Hopeless
  - Trapped
  - A sense of failure
  - Dislike for your child
  - Fear that you'll never be able to cope
  - Fear that you might hurt your child
  - Too frantic to think straight

Most parents in the world, especially new mothers are likely to feel a few such moments of bleak misery at one time or another. But it is important to recognise these feelings and tell someone. Talking them out with a trusted person can really help.

- The anxiety we feel as parents may link directly back to our own babyhood and childhood experiences.
- There may be other problems in our lives making the situation worse.
- Many parents feel lonely, isolated, even imprisoned with a crying baby.

- Try to remember that this stage is not going to last forever. It will get easier as your baby grows and becomes more aware of herself and

	Mon	Tues	Wed	Thurs	Fri	Sat	Sun
Morning	7 to 7.25 Fed her	6.45 to 7.10 Fed early	6.50 to 7.20 Fed her	-	6 to 6.35 Fed her	7 to 8 Fed her	7.35 to 8 Put carry cot in kitchen. Shut door
Morning	9 to 9.35 Rocked in pram	9.05 to 9.40 Rocked in pram	9.20 to 10 Rocked & jiggled		9.15 to 10.15 Rocked in pram	11.10 to 11.30 Rocked in pram	
Afternoon	4 to 4.20 Picked her up — 5.30 to 6 Stroked head. Left her.	1.10 to 2 Rocked in pram — 3 to 3.20 Left her to cry in the yard	4 to 4.35 Extra feed	Rocked in pram — 3.40 to 5.15 Left her to cry	1 to 1.45 Radio full blast	2 to 2.30 Rocked in pram — 4 to 4.45 Rocked in pram	12.10 to 1.15 Screamed on and off. — 3.30 to 3.50 Jiggled
Evening	8 to 9.30 Screaming. Held her. Rocked in pram.	7.05 to 8.15 Screaming Tried everything Shouted at her.	7.20 to 8.10 Carried around. Radio full on.	~ ~	7 to 7.25 Stroked head — 7.55 to 8.20 Jiggled, carried	9.15 to 9.40 On lap. Turned TV volume up..	8.15 to 9 Screaming Rocked in pram
Night	11.45 to 12.15 Stroked head — 3.15 to 4 Into our bed. Fed her.	12.30 to 12.45 Fed her — 4 to 4.35 Fetched her into our bed. Fed her.	10.10 to 11 Swinging carry cot on & off. — Talking to her	10 to 11 Jiggled. Walked about. — 1 to 1.30 3 to 3.20 Left her to cry.	10.45 to 11.10 Screaming Extra feed. — 1.15 to 3 On & off. Left her to cry.	12.10 to 12.45 Fed again — 4 to 4.20 Fed again.	10.15 to 10.55 Fed again — 1.35 to 2.05 Fed again. Talked to her. Into our bed

the world around her, and is able to communicate her needs.

- Try to look after yourself as well as your baby. Take a little time to do things you enjoy.
- Find someone to talk to; a friend, relative, counsellor, doctor or nurse. Parentline and CRY-SIS provide telephone helplines for parents with distressed and crying babies and toddlers (addresses and telephone numbers in the Resources List at the end of this book).
- Keep a Crying Diary. It will help you take a step back and get an accurate picture of what is happening

Older Babies

(over 6 months)

Helping Your Child
Sleep Through the Night

Now your baby is 6 months old or so, he is watching, listening and trying to join in with life around him more and more every day. He is also becoming more attuned to the differences between night and day, and with luck sleeping much longer without a feed at night and enjoying bigger meals during the day. It is now time to encourage a rhythm to the day where the baby wakes and sleeps in a regular pattern and begins to learn calming and settling habits of his own to take him off to sleep. Helping your baby develop a healthy sleeping pattern is giving him a gift because it will be so valuable to him in the long run.

The first comforts you give to your newborn baby are through the gentle ways you feed him, handle him and soothe him. These ways become comforting habits for both of you. But now he is older he needs the first, very gentle touch of discipline in his life, which is that of a routine or rhythm for naps and for bedtime. This is the first

big step. If you don't already have a routine, 6 months is the time to start. He will quickly get used to the pattern you set and his body clock will begin to respond to it. Develop a shape for the day that suits you both. Watch his eyes and see when he looks sleepy. Take the hint. He may naturally be more inclined to nap either in the morning, or the afternoon, or both. As he grows older and needs less sleep and more fun, you can change the shape of the day accordingly, as you read the signs of his needs and progress.

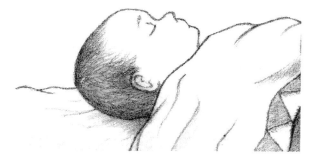

Daytime settling

For most people, it's easier to work first on the daytime routine when you are less tired and more able to be clear-headed and firm. Then you can do the same at night as soon as you feel ready for it.

You can begin to encourage your baby to learn to settle himself to sleep without your help. This is a gradual process. He will need plenty of time to adjust to each new change in his routine. Here are some suggestions:

- Begin to have an interval between feeding him and lying him down to sleep, so that he is not sucking himself to sleep.
- No more rocking or pushing *to get him to sleep* as you did when he was younger. Rock him and push him at *other times* of the day.
- No more singing or talking *at going to sleep times*. Sing to him and cuddle him *before* you lie him down in his sleeping place.

- No more shaking of rattles or waving of toys to distract him after he has been laid down to sleep and starts to cry.
- When he shows the first signs of drowsiness, lay him down in his bed. He needs to get used to falling asleep by himself. If he cries himself back into wakefulness, go to him and soothe him, but once he is drowsy again, return him to his cot and gently take your leave. Don't let him fall asleep in your arms, or with your hand stroking him. If you do, he will miss the feeling and cry whenever he wakes to find you gone. He will come to depend on your soothing for falling asleep.
- Only return to the use of earlier comforting habits of helping him to sleep when he is ill.
- Make sure his cot or bed is comfortable and welcoming. It is right to keep the beds of very young babies free of padded items as a precaution against suffocating. Now that your baby can move around, you may want to add a cuddly toy or a special soft blanket to make him feel safe and cocooned.
- Persevere!

Sooner or later, your baby will begin to develop settling habits of his own because you have given him the chance to learn to do so on a firm and regular basis. He will learn to snuggle down, shut his eyes, perhaps suck his fist or thumb or stroke a soft blanket or cuddly toy and sink into drowsiness, then sleep. Other babies develop habits like 'talking' to themselves, rocking themselves, or twirling their hair with two fingers.

Bedtime

There is already, in everyone's body, a going-to-sleep mechanism waiting to be properly used. We fall asleep as our body temperature falls to its minimum and we awake as our body temperature begins to rise again, our body having rested enough. But we need to help the system by going along with it. We need an unwinding routine each bedtime, and the darkness, quiet and comfort that is right for the night.

By 6 months your baby is no longer his own little microclimate with its own calms and raging storms. He is sensitive to whatever is going on around him now, stimulated by sound and sight, and capable of being lulled by peace and quiet. You need to watch out for his responses and try to give him the conditions he needs to turn tiredness into sleep.

At bedtime follow the same steps for settling your baby to sleep as you did in the daytime. However, you may also want to add a special 'goodnight' ritual before you lie him down – sing a song, say a blessing, chant a rhyme, kiss a favourite toy, or say 'goodnight' to other members of the family. These rituals can be a comfort to everyone – but keep them very short and simple.

Night-time waking

The night can be a tense time for us because we are longing to sleep ourselves. We believe that if our child wakes and cries, there must be something wrong, so we will always find an excuse for him: 'He's teething'. 'He's catching a cold'. 'He's too hot.' But, by this age, almost always, it is more habit than anything else which causes your baby to wake. The greater the efforts we make to help a child get back to sleep, the more attention he gets from us, the more he may wake, expect it, and cry for it.

A great help for settling babies at night is to make a strong contrast between how you respond to him during the day and how you respond to him at night. Give him maximum attention during the day when he is awake, alert and responsive. Give him absolutely minimum attention at night. Cut down your smiles. No talk. No eye contact. Just absolute quiet, and gentle hands touching him as little as possible and only to do the essential things such as nappy changing and lifting him out of, and putting him back into, his sleeping place. Have everything you might need within arms' reach.

Reassurance

If you have difficulties settling him to sleep and resettling him when he wakes and cries for you during the night, try this method of reassurance:

1 Dim the lights.
2 Sit silently beside him, no talking, no eye contact, no movement until he falls asleep. If his crying makes you feel so desperate you have to pick him up, try standing by the cot holding him, with as little movement and sound as possible, until he calms down. Then settle him back.
3 Each night, move the chair you sit on further away from his cot to distance your body from him a step at a time – until you can walk straight out of the room as soon as you have laid him down. Alternatively, spend a few moments walking quietly round the room, tidying up – then slide out of the door.

Ideally, don't get him out of his cot after bedtime unless you think something is wrong.

If possible, avoid

- putting a screaming baby in the car and driving round half the night – unless, perhaps, you have an angry, sleepless neighbour on the other side of the wall;
- giving him a bottle each time he wakes up crying, maybe six times in the night! Try a few sucks of water if you are longing to give him something. He may be grateful or disgusted! Don't give in, he'll soon learn that water is the only night-time drink provided – and his tummy will get the message too;
- rocking or pushing the baby to sleep in the pram. Unless you are desperate, follow the same pattern as you have practised for his rest-time settling down.

Once again, persevere

It will take time for your baby to grow comfortable with a new, stricter, regime! It will be well worth it. Helping your baby establish a healthy sleeping/waking pattern will set the stage for good sleep for the rest of his life.

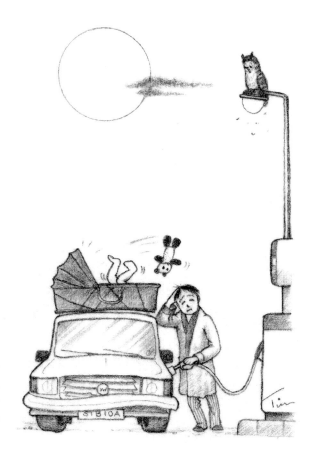

Ill babies

When your baby is unwell, don't concern yourself with the usual routine. Instead, snuggle up together; he needs you close. In this special circumstance, you may want to try some of the soothing methods you used in his first 6 months. They may be very comforting to him when he is feeling uncomfortable all over and crying with distress.

Sharing the settling

Children quickly learn to exploit the different reactions they get from different people.

Whether your child is eight months or three years old, it will be easier and quicker to settle him if you and your partner plan and work out strategies together so you can both stick to them without fail. If you are on your own, there may be someone else who helps you from time to time. Share the same approach to settling your child, so that he recognises the pattern. Tell your toddler what you are going to do, and do it. Tell him what he is and is not allowed to do and both stick to it as firmly as you can. As before, be consistent and stand united.

'Stand united'

Can't sleep, won't sleep!

What if you have done all the things suggested above, persevered with them, and your 6+ months baby still won't go to sleep without a big fuss – or stay asleep?

If your baby was settling fairly well but has suddenly become disturbed again there may be a physical cause, such as the onset of illness or teething. Check his temperature and his nappies. Diarrhoea often goes with teething.

If your baby has never settled well or if the problem continues without other symptoms, then you are facing a baby who simply cannot or will not accept that he needs to go to sleep alone. He may cry himself into a screaming fit at bedtime, wake in the night for more prolonged bouts of screaming, and end up having to make up for lost sleep during the day – which probably means more wakefulness the next night. This can leave parents feeling exhausted, angry, anxious, and miserable. It is often more difficult to settle children who are still too young to talk. Their efforts to communicate fail, so they cry and then cry louder as they sense our rising tension.

Ways forward

Whether the problem of waking and crying has always been impossible to solve, or whether the trouble has suddenly started up again, there are still all kinds of ways forward for you.

Ways forward may in fact mean going backwards for a while and repeating the same calming and settling pattern you used to use when your baby was younger. If those ways became familiar and comforting then, they may help now to renew the sense of security in him that might have evaporated as a result of the present build-up of tension between you at night. Go back to your own old favourites and try them again.

Stroking and rocking

Many parents return to soothing their baby asleep by stroking or rocking him as they did when he was little. It often works but it can be a very short-term answer. It relies on you being free to do the stroking and rocking each time, and being able to keep it up for as long as he needs. Some older babies who fall asleep like this feel panicky later on when they stir or half-wake and realise that the comforting movement has stopped. They may even start to wake and cry more frequently, not less. If this is happening, you may need to stop what you are doing and work once again on getting your baby to fall asleep without your comforting touch.

Lying down with your baby

This method involves simply lying down with your baby and pretending to go to sleep yourself. You might hum quietly, or use slow, relaxed breathing to encourage him to sleep. This will often work quite well for an older baby and five or ten minutes lying down may be welcome to you, if you can manage it. The problem with this approach is that you tend to be stuck with it for a long time afterwards. Older babies who grow used to going to sleep like this are very reluctant to give it up. If that's no problem for you at the moment, fine. You will have to help your child go to sleep on his own eventually, but you may feel that getting some regular sleep now, and during the weeks ahead is your top priority.

Brief reassuring visits

Most parents do this quite naturally. They nip in when their baby starts to cry after he has been put to bed, say a word, turn him over perhaps, tuck him in again, stroke his head and leave again quietly and almost immediately. They do this again and again. Otherwise, they may call out from the other room, or downstairs something like: *Quiet now, go to sleep, I'm still here.* This gives reassurance that you are not far away, whilst reinforcing the message that the day has ended and it is time to go to sleep. You may have other ways of your own to help your child to feel safe and loved even when you are not in the same room.

Sleep interruption

Some parents whose babies wake and cry at the same time each night after they have been weaned have found they can change the habit by half-waking him up themselves. The trick is to go to the baby *before* he wakes and begins to fuss.

Between fifteen minutes and an hour before he usually wakes and cries, the parents go to him and gently stir him half out of sleep with their hands. Immediately they settle him down again and say softly 'Go back to sleep now'. With some babies, this is enough to break the pattern of regular waking, and they soon begin to sleep through the usual wake-up patch. Once the habit is broken, the parents can stop the sleep interruption visits.

Note This must be done very gently so that it is not a harsh or unpleasant experience for the baby. If it doesn't help after five nights, leave it.

RED FLAG WAVING!

Check and Ignore. Right from the Start has strong reservations about this approach and does **not** recommend it. However, some parents use it and it does stop some babies crying, but the cost to the child might well be high. Check and Ignore involves just what it says: parents go quickly to the baby when he wakes and cries, check that he is not ill and change his nappy if necessary. They do not talk to him or soothe him at all but leave immediately and let him cry alone for as long as it takes for him to fall asleep again. No one can really tell what sense of abandonment, distress or fear might remain in the mind of a child after being left to cry at night like this, entirely without comfort, nor what the effect might be on his developing personality.

Timed Settling

The Timed Settling routine is very different from Check and Ignore. It is a respectful, careful, yet still very firm and precise way of helping an older baby, toddler, or young child learn to sleep through the night without his mum's or his dad's presence, and all the attention, drinks and cuddles that go with it. It is a routine that can ease a 9 month-old baby into a peaceful sleep pattern before bad habits have a chance to develop. It is also easier to use the Timed Settling routine with a baby this age than with a more active and determined toddler.

Timed Settling needs a detailed introduction and explanation and thoughtful planning, as well as advice and support from your health visitor or community nurse before you undertake it. For these reasons, and because the technique can be used to help any child from 9 months to 3 years we have placed it in a separate chapter of its own.

You may want to go straight to Chapter 6 now to discover what Timed Settling is all about and see whether you think it might help you and your older baby if he is still unsettled and causing problems at night, despite whatever else you have tried to settle him. Timed Settling is something that not all parents will want to go for, in which case they can just leave Chapter 6 aside. When you read about Timed Settling in detail your instinct will tell you whether it feels right for you and your child.

What if none of these strategies have helped?

You may have tried everything suggested here; or also have moved on to Chapter 6 and, with the support of your health visitor, tried the Timed Settling routine. If nothing has made any big difference to your child's wakefulness, even after dogged perseverance, it may mean that your child is unique in one particular way. He knows he desperately needs to be physically close to you at night because he is not yet emotionally ready to sleep on his own – perhaps not for another year or so. There are just a very few children whose distress at this separation at night from their mothers cannot be borne or overcome through any means. If this is true for your child, you will come to recognise it within two weeks of starting to use the Timed Settling method. In which case, a mattress by your bed, his cot tied alongside or a big enough bed to include him is the only solution there is. It usually proves, after the acclimatisation period, to be a very comforting one. Many parents look back on all the struggles they went through and recognise that this in the end was the best decision they ever made.

Getting together with other parents

Try to link up with other parents who are going through the same exhausting struggles, so you can compare your experiences and report progress. This sharing of the heartache and the challenge quickly lessens the lonely load that parents bear and gives a big lift of encouragement. It turns feelings of despair into a shared effort, and, for the first time, gives everyone a chance to chuckle over the nightmare you have been living through.

In a nutshell

- When a baby is 6 months old or so, it is time to help him develop a regular sleeping pattern. Learning to settle himself into sleep, and sleep in a regular rhythm will set the stage for healthy sleep for the rest of his life.
- Begin by establishing a daily routine for naps and for bedtime. He will quickly get used to the pattern you set and his body clock will begin to respond to it.
- Encourage your baby to settle himself to sleep by removing, one at a time, any comforts that you have been using to stop him crying and settle him to sleep. Gradually, *he will begin to develop settling habits of his own.*
- Only return to earlier comforting habits when he is ill or if he goes through a bad patch.
- At bedtime follow the same steps for settling your baby to sleep as you did in the daytime. However, add a special 'goodnight' ritual before you lie him down.
- Give maximum attention during the day and minimum attention at night.

- Sit silently beside him, without talking, eye contact or movement. Each night gradually move your chair further away from the cot, until you can eventually just leave the room.
- Try not to lift him out of his cot unless you think something is wrong.
- Avoid driving him around in the car, giving him a bottle when he cries in the night, and rocking or pushing him to sleep in the pram: he will become dependent on these things for falling asleep.
- Look out for physical causes of sleeplessness, such as the onset of illness or teething.
- Try these ways forward if you are having sleep problems: stroking and rocking, lying down with your child, giving reassurance either verbally or by brief visits, sleep interruption, and Timed Settling (see Chapter 6).
- Check and Ignore is a further method, but not one which we recommend.
- Try to link up with other parents who are going through the same difficulties. It can turn feelings of despair into a shared effort.

Timed Settling
(from 9 months to 3 years old or so)

We all have a slipping-into-sleep mechanism waiting to be used each night. Timed Settling is a disciplined approach to encourage your child's natural sleeping mechanism to work well. It gives parents a firm framework to use that teaches their child to give up ingrained habits of waking and crying for them during the night, and to recover peaceful sleep patterns, which are every child's birthright.

Timed Settling helps a child to pick up the knack of falling asleep on her own. It involves leaving a child, once settled into bed for the night, to cry for short periods and then, if necessary, for slightly longer periods of time. *It means always returning to comfort her silently, lovingly but very briefly at regular intervals, without ever lifting her out of her sleeping place.* It means comforting your child by touch, briefly and silently, again … and again … and again … night after night, for a while. It hardly ever needs more than a week of this controlled and steady response to bring back undisturbed nights and peace for everyone.

How did Timed Settling develop?

The Timed Settling routine was originally developed instinctively by mothers who had become so shattered by broken nights and sleep starvation that they began to try out other ways of persuading their older babies or toddlers to change the bad habits they had got into. They tried all kinds of strategies and found that one, firmer, more precise step-by-step method worked particularly well to bring peace back into their lives in a very short time and allow their children to develop a natural, healthy sleep pattern. Because Timed Settling can help babies, toddlers and young children to sleep undisturbed, they begin to feel happier and more secure.

Since the early 1990s this strategy, amongst others, has been researched and recommended by doctors, paediatricians, child psychologists and child and family care workers and used by them as a central part of their programmes for supporting and teaching new skills to parents. For example, Tresillian Family Care Centres in Australia have found the Timed Settling routine so valuable that they offer mothers and their crying children a short stay in a residential unit, if they need that professional help and encouragement right beside them during the night, to undertake the Timed Settling routine.

Timed Settling is now being taught by health visitors, community nurses and family care practitioners to hundreds of thousands of mothers in Europe, America and Australia. 'Sleep clinics' are being set up in many places to help parents with their children's sleep problems and support them on a daily basis when they decide to undertake the Timed Settling routine.

> **RED FLAG WAVING!**
> It is very important that you do **not** try the Timed Settling method without the professional involvement of your health visitor, who will take you through this process step by step.

How can Timed Settling help you?

It can prevent a sleep problem developing. It is a routine you can put into practice as soon as you decide that the time has come for your 8 or 9 month old baby to stop waking up several times each night expecting some kind of instant response from you – food, attention or just help in getting back to sleep again. Getting in there early while she is still at the 8–9 month baby stage is sensible, because she will adapt more quickly and easily to the discipline of Timed Settling than if she was older.

It can help when all other techniques have failed to settle your child.

It can be a 'rescue remedy' when the crying has driven you to such a state of despair that you are too confused and angry to think straight any longer. Many parents in this situation feel they might be in danger of hurting their children. Some do so. Timed Settling can be crucial in preventing this from happening.

> The tiredness can make you think you are going mad. It can make you feel ugly all over, inside and out.
>
> *Karin*
>
> I can't even smile at my child during the day any more, I feel so fed up and tired.
>
> *Brittany*
>
> I am just full of dread all day as to what the night will bring.
>
> *Carmel*

Sleep problems in a child invariably mean acute shortage of sleep for one or both parents. The exhaustion and despair that comes from this can put enormous strain on marriages and partnerships, and set the stage for long-term sleep problems for the child. Remember that Timed Settling is in no way a punishment for your child for keeping you awake. By your commitment to it you will be giving your child a gift, the gift of healthy sleep that will last her a lifetime.

Your preparations for Timed Settling

FIRST STEP
Thinking the process through

Read the description of Timed Settling that follows slowly and carefully at least twice and think it through to the end. Imagine yourself undertaking each step of it. Build up a picture of exactly what you would do in your head. 'Feel it through' in your heart. Sleep on it. Only then will you be able to decide whether or not you feel it is right to give it a go.

If you decide 'yes', start by talking through the whole process of Timed Settling with your health visitor and also with a chosen support person at home, whether this is your husband or partner, your mother, sister, or a close friend or neighbour. Give plenty of time to think and talk together about yourself and your own strengths and fears. You will then be able to prepare for action together and later discuss how Timed Settling is working and what you are feeling day by day. If difficult feelings come up for you during the process, or if there are particularly tough moments, your support person will be beside you to steady you, prevent you wavering and joke about the difficulties.

Discuss and adapt the suggestions and instructions that follow to suit your own inclinations and understanding of yourself and your child. Talk it all over with your doctor or health visitor and write down what you have decided to do in terms of the timing to help you stick to it exactly.

SECOND STEP
Other things to think about before you begin

Whether you use the Timed Settling routine with an older baby or with a two or even three year-old, the background is the same, even if the approach may be a little bit different.

Remember that we all cry to release the tension in us. Children instinctively do this immediately and much more often than their parents! If children are *allowed* to cry their times of stress away uninterrupted on your lap or in your arms during the day, they will respond more easily to Timed Settling at night because they will not still be carrying residues of tension waiting to be released.

Remember, when you start to use Timed Settling, it is unavoidable that your child will feel some new stress at not getting quite what she expects from you! She will *need* to cry to release that tension until it has evaporated and she can fall asleep. You will need to be prepared and strong enough to let that crying happen in her cot at night without holding her in your arms to comfort her, as you would normally do during the day time.

Remember that finding ways to calm and steady yourself will be the most crucial part of undertaking the Timed Settling routine successfully to help your child sleep. This is because the tension that has naturally been building up in you with the frustration of trying to cope at night will have got through to her. All children are emotional sponges from day one in their lives. If you are still full of tension when you begin Timed Settling this may make her wake more more often, cry for you more desperately, and take longer to settle back to sleep. *It is essential for you to feel confident and hopeful.* For this reason you will need one hundred percent support from your health visitor and also, ideally, from someone else you trust who can help keep your determination and courage up, especially for the first two or three nights. Being open and sharing any feelings you have of frustration, impatience and anger against your child with someone you trust will help a great deal. You won't so easily feel lonely and overwhelmed.

THIRD STEP
A quick check list before you begin

If she is only 8 or 9 months old, is she completely weaned at night?

Is there a close and warm bond between you (apart from the frustration of her waking and crying at night)?

Do you manage to keep to a reasonably regular routine of feeds, sleeps, play and companionship during the day?

Have you developed a calming, familiar bedtime routine – the same little rituals to enjoy together and to relax each evening before she goes into her bed ?

If there are any boxes you can't tick yet, wait until you can tick them before you undertake the Timed Settling routine. Can you somehow get some help and encouragement for these essentials first?

FOURTH STEP
Check your child's health

It is very important that the Timed Settling method is never put into practice if you suspect your child is not well, because stopping once you have started will be confusing and unhelpful to her. It is essential, therefore, to choose a time when she is in normal, good health. Also, if she is not well when she is put under this new regime, her emotions could be all over the place and she will feel the upset magnified because she's already feeling out-of-sorts and ready to panic and cling.

FIFTH STEP
Bedtime routine

Make sure you have kept the same, familiar, and peaceful bedtime routine going for at least two weeks before you think of starting Timed Settling. Stick to your routine if you possibly can, even if other things have to be delayed or abandoned.

FINALLY
Keep a 'Sleep Diary'

Before you undertake the Timed Settling method it is important and helpful to keep a Sleep Diary for at least ten days along the same lines as the Crying Diary described for a new baby in Chapter 4. This way you will be able to see clearly what is going on each night and how you are responding.

It will help you get on top of the situation, and feel braver about trying something new. On page 75, for example, is the Sleep Diary kept by the mother of Jack (aged 2) a week before she began Timed Settling with him. Jack often took an hour to settle in the evening and then woke and cried again and again during the night. His mother was worn to a shadow, too tired even to visit friends.

You have now prepared yourself well and are ready to get started. However, if your child is already at the toddler stage or older, you will need to prepare her too.

Preparing your toddler or older child for Timed Settling

Children understand an amazing amount of what we are saying, even if they are too young to talk much yet. As soon as you have decided to start the Timed Settling routine with your child choose a peaceful moment during the day – not when it is almost bedtime – and tell her about the changes to come. Don't repeat it. Just tell her once. Something will begin to sink in. This respects her intelligence and begins to prepare her a little for the new routine ahead.

Tell her clearly and matter-of-factly that she is a big girl now and it's time to learn to sleep peacefully at night and not wake up and cry for you.

Tell her that you are going to help her lie down to sleep quietly all night long *just using your hands and no talking.*

Tell her there will be no more bottles at night-time, or whatever other tactics you have been using to try to quieten things.

You may have the additional problem of a toddler old enough to climb out of bed ten times a night to come and find you. The only way to achieve a Timed Settling routine in such a situation is to be brave enough to make the whole room her 'bed'. You can do this by putting a stair gate or even a safety chain on the door – so the child can see out but not get out – and cushions or small mattress and blanket on the floor for her. This way she can settle herself down finally on her own and can then be moved gently back into her bed later. When she is roaming around crying for you, you can go at the same, timed intervals to reassure her without going into the room, just stroking her head, saying: *Time to sleep,* and leaving her again just as you would do a child in her cot. Quite soon, with luck, she'll be climbing back into her cot on her own to sleep because it's cosier than being on the floor.

Timed Settling
The step-by-step routine

As your health visitor is unlikely to be able to be with you at your child's bedtime and certainly not in the middle of the night, this Right from the Start description of Timed Settling is included here for you and your support person to turn to. Please remember how important it is that you do not just give it a try on your own without discussion and preparation with a trained professional. This description is here for you as a basis for this discussion with your community nurse or health visitor and to use as a guide to help you plan together exactly what you are going to do and to follow it through.

So, here we go. Here is the step-by-step process of Timed Settling – for the next time you hear your baby crying for you after you have settled her down or in the middle of the night.

1 Take a moment

- Take three deep breaths, calm yourself and look at your own hands, before you move.
- Remind yourself that indignant, anxious or impatient thoughts in your mind will go straight to your fingertips and your child will feel it the moment you touch her. If this happens there will be less and less chance to change the stressful habit she has got herself into. Instead, wait for just long enough to bring your most loving memories and thoughts to the surface and hold them there, so that gentleness and patience are there in your hands before you even walk back to your child.

2 Go to her without hurrying

- Say to her quietly and clearly, however old or young she is: 'It's time to sleep', then not another single word.
- Talking just stimulates her brain again. Just make a soothing sound only, or remain completely silent. Try to avoid obvious eye contact. Ask yourself these questions: Has she got a wet nappy? Is she crying from real discomfort or illness or is she just asking for my attention? When you know your child well you can soon tell the difference.
- Decide if anything does need doing and do it. Gently, unhurriedly, lie her down again, tuck her up again, and reassure her just through the firm and loving touch of your hands.
- If she's old enough to be standing up and clinging to the bars of her cot, you may have to lift her up slightly to get her to release her grip, before you turn her around and lie her down. Give her a favourite teddy, dolly or comfort blanket again and keep a hand on her – perhaps stroke her head or rub her tummy or her back in a circle if that proves calming – for a very short time – never more than 15 seconds.
- At this point, the crying may have stopped, may have lessened or may even have increased. It doesn't matter which. Remember that your silent presence for a few seconds is just to reassure her that you have not deserted her and that you love her. She is absorbing that fact in her mind however loudly she is screaming.
- Then, feeling proud of your calm and careful self-control, walk quietly out of the room. Well done! Go straight back to your supporter, to a cup of tea, to watch your television programme, or find anything that will hold your attention for a few minutes.

3 Start watching the clock

- Whether the crying just continues or gets louder – wait for 5 minutes, **not a second less**.
- Then slowly, calmly go back to her and do exactly the same things again, stay not more than 15 seconds and then leave her again. Keep your courage up and have faith. All this is normal. Follow the process no matter how loud and non-stop the crying is.
- Each time you repeat this process, picture your own movements in advance. This way you will have a sure touch each time you go back to resettle her, because you know exactly what you are going to do. You won't be feeling shaky and uncertain, which will stir her up even more.

Sleep Diary of Jack (aged 2)

	Time woke in the morning	Times and lengths of naps during the day	Time went to bed in the evening	Lengths of time to settle to sleep and what you did	Times and lengths of waking at night and what you did
Mon	7.45	11.30 to 12.30	7.30	Cried every few minutes till 8. Settled him down again. 8.15 really screaming. Bottle of fruit juice got him to sleep by 8.45.	12.30 for 5 mins. Sat by him. 3.20 for 8 mins. Gave him a bottle. 4.30 for 8 mins. Reheated bottle. 5.45 for 2 mins. Sat by him.
Tues	7.30	11.30 to 1.15	8.15	Woke up every ten minutes for two hours (not feeling well). Stroked him in his cot or sat him on my lap till he was dozy.	1.15 for 13 mins. Gave him a bottle. 4.24 for 11 mins. Talked to him. Rubbed his head. 6.05 for 18 mins. Wouldn't settle. Took him into our bed.
Wed	6.30	12 to 1.00 In pushchair 3. to 3.20	7.45	Cried and called for 30 mins. Went in and laid him down.	10.45 for 15 mins. 1.15 for 13 mins. 4.24 for 11 mins. 5.40 for 18 mins. Each time, stood by cot till he fell asleep.
Thurs	7.15	11 to 12 in car	8.00	Asleep in 15 mins without any crying.	11pm. Very distressed. Stood by cot. Held his hand for 35 mins. 2.15 changed nappy. Into our bed. An hour to settle.
Fri	6.45	1 to 2.15	7.30	Screamed so loudly, took him out of cot again to watch T.V. till he calmed down. Into bed, asleep by 8.40.	9.40 for 5 mins. Stood over him, stroking his back. 11.45 for 6 mins. Cuddled and talked to him in his cot. 3.50 Screaming. Put him into our bed.
Sat	7.30	2 to 3.20	8.05	Stood up and screamed for an hour. Laid him down and covered him up nine times then left him. Smacked his legs at 9.30 and was really angry. Felt ashamed. He finally slept at 9.45.	11pm for 5 mins. Gave him a bottle of juice. 2am for 50 mins. 4am for 10 mins. Sat with him each time and held his hand.
Sun	7.15	11.30 to 12.15	7.30	Cried for 30 mins. Left him alone.	12 Moaned and cried for an hour. Gave dummy in our bed. Back into cot as soon as asleep. 3.15 cried for 30 mins. Gave him a bottle of milk.

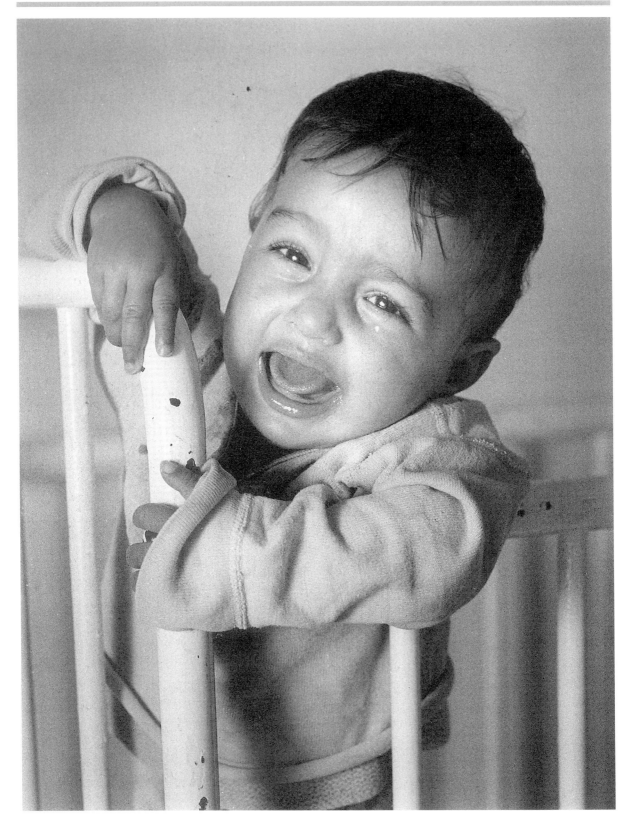

First of all I thought I can't watch the clock like this, it doesn't seem human but then, when I started and was finding it really tough the first three nights I realised that it gives you a kind of framework to hold on to and something else to concentrate on. It really helped me not to panic but to keep calm and control myself. When I think I used to scream and scream at Fred to shut him up at 2 am and kick the leg of his cot, and now all that horror is over after just six nights of Timed Settling. I used to be really scared that the next time he cried in the night I would be hitting him instead of kicking the cot leg.

Seguna

Reminders along the way

- Try your best never to pick her up and lift her out of her cot to hold her in your arms, however much you ache to do so. Even if she works herself up into full blown screaming for a while the first few nights, remember that this will be hurting you far more than it is hurting her. If you pick her up to console her during this learning period, it will probably take three times as long for Timed Settling to work for you. You could find yourself back at square one.
- Don't forget to fill in the Sleep Diary every time you have settled her down again and left her, so you can see, as you persevere each night, when the change begins to come.
- Remind yourself: I'm not just leaving her to cry. I'm leaving her to learn to sleep.
- Relax in any way you can: A cup of tea, music, deep breathing, yoga, meditation. Talk to someone, or your dog or cat, or yourself. Your child may be just crying steadily or having bouts of screaming with pauses to listen for you. Don't give in. Keep an eye on the clock.

Now wait for ten minutes

- If she is still crying, look at your hands again, check the gentleness in them, go back to her and repeat the same gentle, silent process of lying her down, tucking her in, stroking her for the shortest possible time and walking away again without a word said.

If the crying continues ... this time wait for 15 minutes

- Return to her and repeat the process.
- If the waiting is getting too long for you and if you find that your nerves are getting so stretched that you can't bear the build-up of a 15 minute waiting time, play it a little differently. You choose. Perhaps keep it to 5 minute waiting periods on the first night or two, and then build up, night by night, to ten minutes, then fifteen minutes, then twenty minutes. Twenty minutes should be the limit.
- Whatever you decide to do in respect of watching the clock, stick to your decision. You should soon see the change you want.

What is happening?

- During the process, you may hear her fall silent for a few seconds then recover energy for another burst of crying or she may manage to cry without a pause for all that time. Don't worry! This is not damaging her. Crying helps to release tension. She is getting the important messages, which are that you haven't deserted her, that you are still there for her, that you love her and that she is safe. She is also beginning to get the other important message that this is the time for silence and peace and that it would be nicer to be snuggled up and fall asleep than to go on and on struggling to get attention. She is discovering that this is not going to happen; that this is sleeping time.

- If you are lucky, your child may go to sleep after only two or three settlings the first night you try it, or you may have to go back to her five or six times. It may be a two-hour marathon of settling and re-settling her. Don't give up! It may take only two or three nights for peace to come. It may take a week or even ten days with a determined and demanding older child. But people who persevere with this method find that change almost always does come and that it's real and big, and that it lasts. What's more, once you have helped your child do this, you will be able to relax, knowing exactly how to treat any renewal of night disturbances. You will also know that you have taught her a most valuable skill for her life.

- Don't be upset by a sudden burst of longer, louder screaming on the third, fourth or fifth evening. Your toddler may have intelligently recognised that you are imposing a different system at bedtime and is making a last ditch effort to test your resolve and break it down. Try to hold onto the loving determination with which you started. Consider using earplugs if that would help you by taking just the edge off the head-piercing sound of her crying.

One night, it got so bad for me after about eight spaced-out visits to settle him again, I didn't know what I might do next. Just give in, pick him up and carry him out of the room … or belt him. I'd been doing fine until then, but suddenly I felt too screwed up to cope any longer. One second I was feeling heartbroken for him – listening to him crying on and on, the next second I was in such a rage. When I got to the doorway my heart was banging about and I was breathing like I had run up loads of stairs – which we didn't have in our flat anyway. Luckily, I stopped myself before I opened the bedroom door. I just turned back and left him to scream for another minute while I went to the kitchen and slowly drank a whole glass of cold water. You couldn't imagine how that helped! It was like it washed away the confusion and calmed me down so I could go in and do a proper, gentle, settling job with him again after all. That was the turning point too. He went straight to sleep after that for the rest of the night and two nights later he had got himself sorted and was never really a problem again in the night except when he was sick. I never knew till then what a glass of water could do!

Pat

Bedtime routine and Timed Settling working together

Many parents describe the sense of relief they feel at putting themselves 'under orders', without having to be responsible for making further difficult decisions at a shaky time. It also helps them stand back more and wait patiently for the breakthrough, knowing how high the chances are that it will help their child and bring some sanity and sleep back into their own lives.

The second Sleep Diary over the page was made by Jack's mother four weeks after undertaking a steady bedtime routine each night and then the Timed Settling routine as well. She learnt that leaving him like this was leaving him for his intelligence to begin to work … that he would soon begin to grow bored by the effort of more crying … sense that he would not ever get the full attention that he had been crying for … sense that his mum was close by and peaceful even if not in the same room … feel less tense and more secure and at last able to snuggle down and go to sleep by himself.

Jack's mum said afterwards, *My life has got better by 200% and Jack is no longer scratchy and miserable half the day.* As this remark shows, the second major bonus that Timed Settling brings is that it also makes the days easier. Unhappy and bad tempered behaviour in the daytime begins to fade away. The special achievement of Timed Settling is to allow a child's personality to blossom and her interest and enjoyment in everyday happenings to return. Many parents can hardly believe that they alone have brought about all these changes in just a week or two.

Further reading

If you feel you need further information and support about the Timed Settling method you can find it in a small book called *The Good Sleep Guide for You and Your Baby* by Angela Henderson. She calls this method The Sleep Training Programme. This book is now used by many health visitors in the UK and you may be able to borrow a copy; otherwise you will find details in the *Useful Books* list at the end of this book.

Sleep Diary for Jack two weeks after starting the Timed Settling

	Time woke in the morning	Times and lengths of naps during the day	Time went to bed in the evening	Lengths of time to settle to sleep and what you did	Times and lengths of waking at night and what you did
Mon	7.20	11.45 to 12.30 in pushchair	7.30	Cried for a minute. Did nothing.	—
Tues	7.30	11.30 to 12.30	7.45	Asleep in 15 mins. No crying.	—
Wed	7.00	12.00 to 1.15	7.45	Asleep in 25 mins. No crying.	11.30 half an hour. Reassured him without speaking at 11.45 2.00 2 secs
Thurs	6.30	12 to 1.30	7.30	Asleep in 2 mins. No crying.	12.00 2 secs.
Fri	6.15	10 to 10.30	8.10	Fell asleep in my arms.	5.30 2 secs
Sat	6.45	—	8.00	Asleep in ten minutes. Cried for half a minute.	—
Sun	6.45	11.15 to 12	8.10	Chattered to himself for half an hour. Called a few times. Took no notice.	12.30 2 secs

In a nutshell

- We all have, in our bodies, a night time slipping-into-sleep mechanism waiting to be properly used. Timed Settling is a disciplined approach to encourage your child's natural sleeping mechanism to work well.
- Timed Settling helps a child to pick up the knack of falling asleep on her own. It involves leaving a child, once settled into bed for the night, to cry for short periods and then, if necessary, for slightly longer periods of time. **It means always returning to comfort her silently, lovingly but very briefly at regular intervals, without ever lifting her out of her sleeping place.**
- One week of Timed Settling is usually all that is needed to bring back undisturbed sleep.
- Since the early 1990s this strategy, amongst others, has been researched and recommended by doctors, paediatricians, child psychologists and child and family care workers and used by them as a central part of their programmes for supporting and teaching new skills to parents.
- If used early on, Timed Settling can help prevent a sleep problem developing.
- Timed Settling can help when all other techniques have failed to settle your child.
- Timed Settling can be a 'rescue remedy' when the crying has driven you past the point of coping.

- Choose a **medical 'advisor'**. Timed Settling should only be undertaken with the guidance of a doctor, nurse or health care professional familiar with the approach. Though the technique is simple, there is a lot of thought and preparation involved. It needs to be a team effort.
- Choose a **support person**. Timed Settling will require determination, focus and self-control from you. You will need one hundred percent support from your medical advisor and someone else you trust who can help keep your determination and courage up, especially for the first two or three nights.
- Work through the preparation **Steps** described in the chapter with your medical advisor and support person to make sure Timed Settling is right for you and your child. Every step is important.
- Only start Timed Settling when you feel you understand the process thoroughly, have worked through the preparation steps with your medical advisor, and have your support person at the ready.
- **If you can encourage your child to go to sleep on her own, and sleep through the night, you are giving her a gift for life.**

Adult insomnia often links straight back to being unable to settle to sleep and get back to sleep as a child – and not receiving the help needed then.

National Childbirth Trust

Toddlers and Older Children

CHAPTER 7

Toddlers and Sleep

From the age of about 1 year, your child will be much more active – crawling, clambering, pushing, pulling, getting hold of everything within reach and scrambling over you like a monkey up a tree. There is so much more going on in his life and each week he will be getting more and more interested and determined to be involved and to have a go. He'll be staggering all over the place. This often means that switching off and getting to sleep become much harder for him. Sudden removal

from all the excitement and fascination and being put to bed can feel like a serious interruption and therefore very frustrating for him. He may be all set to howl his way to sleep, as often as not.

If a child fights going to sleep, it can be tempting to allow him to go through the day without a nap. But all toddlers need plenty of recouping periods – at least one, if not two daytime naps – if they are not to end up fractious and unhappy by early evening, testing your patience to the limit and maybe beyond. When this happens there may be real trouble brewing for everyone in the house. This is often the reason why some parents look back and say 'Ah! The Terrible Twos!' Sometimes, with a boy, there can be an extra surge of testosterone in his bloodstream at this time. This may give him spurts of headstrong energy and make it more difficult to calm him down on some days. Knowing that this is temporary will help you find extra patience to accept this behaviour.

Most toddlers need between 12 and 14 hours of sleep altogether, with 2 or 3 hours of this total as daytime naps, dwindling away to perhaps one nap of an hour and a half. It is therefore vital that they get enough sleep, at night and by day. They need it for their mental development and well-being. The following chart and a second one in Chapter 8 show how the sleep patterns of babies and toddlers are different from the sleep patterns of older children and adults. Babies and toddlers dream much more than older children. This is nature's way of building up the millions of new brain cell connections needed for the brain's rapid and amazing development at this time.

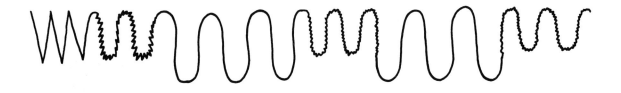

Awake   Drowsy   Deep Sleep   Dreaming   Deep Sleep   Dreaming

Knowledge about babies' sleep patterns and brain activity comes from the research that began as soon as ultrasonic scanning made it possible to watch unborn babies in the womb and record their experiences, their behaviour and their different kinds of brain activity before birth.

Dr Allessandra Piontelli's research, described in her book *From Fetus to Child*, shows how important it is to understand how a baby's brain develops in the womb, and how much dreaming helps in that development. This pattern of deep sleep and then dreaming continues to be important for the first few years of a child's life, while the brain is growing at a great rate. It is therefore valuable to do all we can to help children to find their own, natural sleep patterns during these early years so that their dreaming and deep sleep pattern is not being frequently interrupted.

Helping your toddler settle for a nap

Drowsiness comes on in cycles – every hour or two in young children – and you can learn to watch out for this pattern and pick the right moment to settle your child for his nap or naps.

His now much busier brain needs to slow down into sleepiness for a few moments before you lie him down. When naptime approaches, watch his face and try to notice his reactions. He may be obviously sleepy, or you may need to intervene – to distract his attention and carry him off to unwind for a minute or two. This will give him the chance to relax and become peaceful before the moment comes to lay him down to sleep. It will almost certainly be helpful to remove him firmly but gently from the crowd, or the fun-and-games, a few minutes before his daytime nap.

Take him somewhere quiet if possible, accept calmly any brief fury that erupts – take no notice of it at all – and sit him on your lap to 'talk' to a cuddly toy or look at a picture book or family photographs together. Kiss and rock him. Sing or hum to him. If he is thrashing too much on your lap, carry him round the room slowly and calm him down by showing him something that will interest him, or look out of the window together. Then, if you can, lie him down at more or less the same time each day so that his 'body clock' can fall into the pattern you are setting.

Helping your toddler wake from a nap

Whether or not to wake your child from his nap, or to allow him to wake when he is ready depends on the child's individual need for sleep and the time of day. If your child tends to nap in the morning, it may be fine to leave him to wake when he is ready. However, a long sleep late in the day can mean a much later bedtime and little chance for adult peace in the evening.

Some toddlers, but not all, feel crotchety and miserable for quite a while if they are woken up from a deep sleep in the daytime. However, if you choose to wake him when you think he has had a long enough nap, you can try different ways of waking him slowly and gently to see which work best.

- First use your voice, talking or singing quietly
- Then use your touch – stroke his head, his tummy or his back
- Then lift him and sit with him quietly so he can re-absorb the life going on around him
- Then give him a drink of water or a nibble of fruit to help clear his head

Bedtime

Bedtime can feel like a very big separation for a toddler. His imagination may be just beginning to be very active and he may become frightened by things that did not affect him before. At the same time, he is talking more and wanting to share everything with his parents and be within close reach of one or the other for help, encouragement and fun, every waking moment. He will need to be eased into settling into bed with calm reassurances, lots of touch and cuddles and the comfort of a familiar and peaceful routine beforehand, even if that routine gets interrupted sometimes.

The bedtime routine is even more important than the naptime wind-down. It needs to signal that the whole household is going into a different phase, so that your toddler comes to associate it with a long night's sleep. Toddlers are less adaptable than babies. They like the security of doing the same things in the same way each evening.

Do you have a winding down routine and a regular bedtime each night?

If bedtimes are usually haphazard and sometimes tense times for everyone, you could use the following pattern until you have had time to think out your own, depending on how many tired children, jumping dogs, boiling pans, and how much time you have on your hands.

1 **Getting ready for bed**. Make a routine for the last preparations for bed: washing or bathing, changing into night clothes, putting things away in their proper places for the night, will all help your child to unwind at the end of the day. Being in warm water is special. Do whatever you do in the same order, as much as you can most nights.

2 **Create a ritual**. Decide upon two or three little, symbolic, closing-down activities to share together, also completed in the same order each night. For instance:
   - Look at a picture book or read a story… preferably rather repetitive, with pictures and poetic descriptions. Opt for something comforting rather than exciting. And keep it firmly to one story only (to cut out any manipulation and begging for more by an older child).
   - Tell a story of your own, with your child on your lap, if possible. Talk about the day that has just passed and plans for tomorrow.

- Walk once round the room, holding the child, to say 'goodnight' to the pictures on the wall, to favourite toys, to the sky, the trees, the grass, the buildings, or streetlights outside. Always slowly, gently and quietly.
- Sing a favourite song or say a prayer or a rhyming jingle. Let the child choose if old enough.

3 **Then into bed**. A last kiss, cuddle or stroke then put the child's chosen 'cuddly' (special toy, piece of cloth or whatever has become favourite) into the child's hands just before you walk away and leave the room. Have this special comforter ready for this moment.

After about three weeks the step-by-step routine will have become a familiar and comforting pattern, which relaxes everyone at the end of the day. Try not to hurry. Enjoy the rhythm of it. This can start as early as you like, and can be adapted as the child grows and develops.

Dawn

Try to get in there before the crying really starts!

Avoid leaving an early-waking toddler until he is crying and screaming for you. This will then become his habit. It teaches him that he has to cry in the morning to get your attention. Once he realises that you will go in when he is not crying, with luck, it will become possible to leave him for a little longer. The child feels calm and relaxed instead of working himself into a frenzy. If he wakes up horribly early, keep very quiet yourself. Say nothing at all or just the barest minimum. 'Shhh ... everyone is still asleep! It's still night time! Go back to sleep.' Perhaps give him a toy or two or a book and a small drink, and leave him again immediately. Often a toddler, if left like this, will play for a short while and fall asleep again until breakfast time and the sounds of everyone getting up.

When sleep problems continue

No two children are the same in their need for sleep, or in the way their sleep patterns respond to the changes and pressures of their age. Toddlers in particular can seem at variance with themselves as well as with the rest of the world. Sleep disturbances in a toddler can seem utterly random and bewildering, but there are certain basic things you can check out, to help you respond.

● **Is he feeling unwell?**
Young children often feel 'off-colour' for a while. This can lead to bouts of unexpected tears throughout the day and distress at bedtime. An unwell child instinctively wants to be held close and not left to bear the uncomfortable sensation alone.

As toddlers are not really old enough to describe what they feel, it is up to you to try to recognise those days when he is not really well. It's easy not to notice and to feel cross instead of sympathetic! If he is showing no definite symptoms, like a high temperature, but you feel he is under the weather, give him as much quiet time with you as you can

'Watch his face'

manage. This will allow him to rest and unwind. And you will be better able to spot any symptoms that do develop.

Has something made him anxious or frightened?

Very young children may be made anxious by things that their parents assume they will not understand – such as family changes and stresses like illness, moving house, or arguments between their parents. A big trauma like a parental break-up is bound to affect a toddler, but even smaller changes like a parent going away on a work trip may be unsettling. Even seeing something scary on television can deeply upset a young child. The child's anxieties can stay with them throughout the day and then resurface at night.

If you think something is upsetting your child, watch his face and listen to him. Be willing and ready to stop and listen when he begins to cry, without interrupting his tears. When the crying stops, try to find out what has upset him. Do some guessing to help him. Talk about it quietly. Once he has faced it often enough, it will lose its power to unsettle him and wake him in the night. Drawing, painting and play-acting can also help a young child face a difficult issue and release his anxiety.

If he is too young to talk or to understand your careful explanations, use lots of comforting touch, or bath together, or draw pictures for him of the changes that have happened or the changes to come. Encourage him to draw his own pictures too. He will begin to feel more in control of the situation and less confused and frightened. Sticking to a familiar routine each evening helps most of all to minimise a child's anxiety.

Is there a new baby in the family?

Some toddlers and young children look on with growing fascination at a new baby, especially when the gurgling, kicking and smiling begin, but for others, the new arrival can be a disaster. It can mean his first experience of acute and continuing distress and anxiety – as if his own mother has been taken over. The pangs of jealousy may be so overwhelming that he cannot handle the pain of it. Screaming tantrums or abject misery may take over so forcefully that it can seem like watching his personality change.

For most children, this time of acute jealousy will fade quite quickly if it is accepted with understanding and sympathy. Extra affection, tactful distractions, and inventive efforts to share baby-care responsibilities as much as possible for just a minute or so at a time, can soon begin to melt the icy grip of jealousy. A daily rhythm or routine is all the more important to provide the child with secure boundaries, and a sense of familiarity in amongst all the changes around him. Playfully role-playing the changes can also help.

There are lots of detailed suggestions to help you give comfort to a very jealous child in the Right from the Start book called *Calmer, Easier, Happier Parenting*.

Is he frightened of the dark?

Often, without realising it, we may sow the seed of fear of the dark in a child by asking 'Do you want the light on?' The child wonders why – and begins to find reasons to dislike the dark. If this has happened, you may need to organise a dim light of some kind. Remove anything that is spooking him. Cuddle and soothe him until you can feel him relax in your arms. Give him a special cuddly toy, or look at a favourite picture together. You can say things like: *It's all right! I'm not far away. Don't worry. I'm here. I'm not leaving you alone.*

Is he feeling lonely?

The instinct to stay in close touch with adults day and night is strong, particularly in sensitive and imaginative children. Most children sleep better when they are within earshot of the comforting background noises of ordinary human hubbub. It can be counter-productive to say 'Sssh!! Be quiet!! She's trying to get to sleep!' Sudden sounds out of nowhere will then startle the child awake again. If a child associates going to bed with being totally cut off from his carers, his thoughts and emotions may begin to run round in circles and keep him awake. A few reassuring words can help: *I'll hear you if you call me.' 'I'll always look after you.'*

● **What is going on inside?**
Is he eating enough varied, fresh and natural food? Has he eaten something sustaining and easy to digest for his last meal of the day, not just sugary food and drink? Is he eating food he could be allergic to or which contains those additives that can cause mental disturbance and hyperactivity and keep him tossing and turning all night? (The Right from the Start book *Food For Thought* could help here.)

● **If he is at playgroup or nursery school, is something there upsetting or over-whelming him?**
Is there even a small element of dread of the next morning? Explore this possibility by talking to him and to his teachers.

● **Could the change of seasons be affecting him?**
We all need less sleep in summer, more in the winter. Adults often deny this fact and just go by habit, electric lighting and the clock all the

'Behaviour problems caused by food additives?'

year round. Children know better! You may need to adapt your day to match children's early summer waking – or make very thick curtains to shut out the light and bluff them into sleeping longer. Children forced to spend too long in bed become frustrated and learn to dislike their sleeping place.

- **Do you ever put your child in bed as a punishment for disruptive behaviour?**
  If so, he may begin to associate his bed with punishment and so could automatically tense up every time you put him there. Could you think of another place for him to cool off? Beds should have happy associations. Hiding little surprises occasionally in a child's bed has a wonderful effect.

- **Have you changed your child's bedtime routine?**
  Sometimes it is necessary to change the bedtime routine. For instance, if your child has been used to you staying with him while he falls asleep, it eventually becomes necessary to detach yourself and start helping your toddler to settle himself to sleep. Because toddlers like and need the security of repetition, your child may rebel at any changes and be difficult to settle. You will need to recognise this and persevere gently until he has adjusted to the new routine.

- **There's no problem, I'm just awake**
  Some toddlers go through phases of waking up for an hour or so each night, not crying necessarily, but full of energy and wanting to play. There's nothing wrong; they're just wakeful. This can take a terrible toll on parents. If you've been through all the possible causes, and tried all the remedies, and your child is still waking in the small hours ready to take on all comers, the only thing you can do is try to work out strategies for minimising disruption and maximising your own sleep. Here is a list collected from parents who have been through this:

- I put on a story tape for him to listen to in bed.

  Janet

- We made a rota and took it in turns really strictly … that way at least one of us got a good night's sleep.

  Rich and Susan

- I used to organise longer and more energetic outdoor activities with as much walking and running as possible so he would be more relaxed at night and need more sleep. Wherever I went, I looked for hills!

  Cheri

- I am silent and boring at all times between 9pm and 7am.

  Rhisa

If this goes on for long, you may need to seek help, or reassurance, from your doctor or other medical staff. The phase will end eventually.

In a nutshell

As your toddler becomes more and more interested and involved in life, he may find it increasingly difficult to switch off and go to sleep.

- Most toddlers need between 12 and 14 hours of sleep altogether, with 2 or 3 hours of this total as daytime naps, dwindling away to perhaps one nap of an hour and a half. It is therefore vital that they get enough sleep, at night and by day. They need it for their mental development and well-being.

- Develop a **wind-down routine** for settling your toddler for a nap. As closely as possible to the same time each day, take him to a quiet place and do something relaxing together, perhaps look at a picture book, sing or hum a song, or rock in a rocking chair. Create a routine and follow it each day before you put him to bed.

- Whether or not to wake your child from his nap, or to allow him to wake when he is ready depends on the child's individual need for sleep and the time of the day. If you need to wake your child from his nap, do so very slowly and gently, using first your voice and then your touch.

- The **bedtime routine** is even more important than the naptime wind-down. Toddlers like the security of doing the same things in the same way each evening. Try to follow a routine closely and include some little rituals that he can come to associate with the transition to bedtime.

- In the morning, try to get there before the crying starts so that he does not feel he needs to cry for your attention.

- When sleep problems continue, asking yourself these questions may help you identify the cause:

  - Is he feeling unwell?
  - Has something made him anxious or frightened?
  - Is there a new baby in the family?
  - Is he frightened of the dark?
  - Is he lonely?
  - What is going on inside? (diet etc)
  - If he is at playgroup or nursery school, is something there upsetting or overwhelming him?
  - Could the change of seasons be affecting him?
  - Do you ever put him in bed as a punishment for disruptive behaviour?
  - Does he have happy associations with his bed?

- Have you changed his bedtime routine?

  - Some toddlers go through phases of waking up for an hour or so at a time each night, full of energy and wanting to play. There's nothing wrong; they're just wakeful. You may have to find ways to cope with this wakefulness.

A child has a right to cry even for a stone.

Janusz Korczak

CHAPTER 8

As Children Grow Older

Bedtime can mean many things to older children. When all is going well it can be a special part of the day. Ideally it brings them:

- security
- warmth and comfort
- shared quiet time with a parent, grandparent or carer
- closeness and affection
- relaxation
- a pleasant sensation of being cocooned
- the casting off of the busy-ness of the day

But when things go wrong, children may experience:

- loneliness – 'Why don't they want me around?'
- stress – 'I can't go to sleep and I'm going to be in trouble.'
- anxiety – fears or worries carried over from the day.
- discomfort – too hot/too cold/thirsty/hungry.
- conflict and tension – being told: 'Just shut up and go to sleep!'

Older children will have their ups and downs with sleeping, just as they did when they were babies and toddlers. The atmosphere and habits surrounding bedtime can quickly form either a friendly or a vicious circle. In this chapter, we will look at the sleep patterns of older children, what problems may arise, and what we can do to encourage happy and healthy sleeping habits.

Sleep patterns in older children

Older children and adults have three stages of sleep instead of only two: deep sleep, light sleep and dreaming sleep. They sleep deeply early in the night, move in and out of light sleep and dreaming sleep during most of the night, and then sleep deeply again before dawn. In either light sleep or dreaming sleep, especially if part of the dream startles them, children come right to the surface, like a little fish to the surface of a pond, and may come fully awake for a few seconds before sinking down again into deep sleep or renewed dreaming. They normally therefore half-wake and move around more often during the night than a baby does.

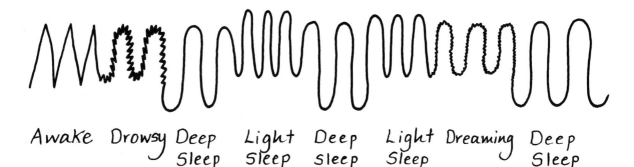

Awake   Drowsy   Deep Sleep   Light Sleep   Deep Sleep   Light Sleep   Dreaming   Deep Sleep

I don't want to go to bed

If, when you have put your child to bed, she's soon up again and coming to find you, or waking frequently in the night, it might be time to look again at the bedtime routine. Are you still following a bedtime routine? Perhaps it needs adjusting according to the child's changing needs, as she grows older. Has a sudden change in the routine disrupted her going-to-sleep habits?

It may be possible to solve problems by adjusting something quite simple – leaving the bedroom door partly open, for instance, so your child doesn't feel isolated. Or perhaps she simply needs less sleep now and feels genuinely frustrated at being put to bed when she still feels full of life. It may be appropriate to adjust her bedtime for her age and energy level. Or perhaps

'It's the boys who seem to wander downstairs most often for reassurance'

you can try organising a wind-down activity for her to do alone in her bed. Depending on her age, she could read or listen to a story on tape, listen to music, or do some colouring, or another peaceful activity to help her relax.

If you have fallen out of the habit of a bedtime routine because of a growing family, working hours or other pressures on you, it is worth every effort to try to restore it. If the old routine has become stale to the child, think how you might change it. Perhaps replace the story with ten minutes quiet colouring together or some other calming activity that gets things ready for tomorrow.

If the 'I don't want to go to bed' habit means your child has been staying up later than you want her to, you can gently nudge her back to an earlier bedtime. Simply begin your twenty-minute winding down process close to the time when she has been settling. Then bring this slowly forward by 10–15 minutes each week until you have set bedtime at the hour you need it to be. If you meet resistance, be strong, just say gently but firmly: *It's time to sleep*, and lie her down.

If she has slipped into a pattern of staying awake later *and* sleeping late the next day, you will need to shift her wake-up time by getting her awake and out of bed 15 minutes earlier than usual for several days, and only then bringing forward her bedtime to match. You may need to make three or four 15-minute shifts, one at a time, to rearrange her sleeping pattern fully.

Regardless of the cause, when your child reappears after having been put to bed, it is best to be matter-of-fact and quick in dealing with it. Accept her appearance calmly, always go to her at once and slowly lead her, in silence, straight back to bed, perhaps via the toilet and a sip of water. Remind her of the time, give a word of comfort and stay with her for a moment of reassurance before leaving her again. Repeat the same process again whenever it happens, so she knows that, once in bed, she will not be able to slip back into daytime activities.

If nothing seems to make any difference and she is still unable to settle or to sleep through the night without coming to find you, it's time to search for a wider cause. What happens to children during the day will always affect their emotional state and this in turn will affect how they go to sleep – and whether they sleep through the night.

> You may want to consider adding a rest time to your child's daily routine. Children who have a quiet and peaceful period in the middle of the day often sleep better and for longer at night. This is probably because of the calmer atmosphere that comes with it and the steadying effect of routine.

Looking for Causes of Sleeplessness …

Is there a big worry on her mind?

Older children who keep waking up during the night are most likely to be bearing a load of anxiety which they haven't been able to release. This load may seem trivial to us, but can loom large enough in their minds to prevent them sleeping, or awaken them in the middle of the night. Is she disturbed by something that happened at school... a fear of failure at school...

something she saw in the street... something she saw on television... anger and arguments at home... something she overheard which left a seed of dread in her mind? There are so many possibilities, but the best remedy is to talk about it together, to listen carefully to everything she tells you and never to mock her fears.

When someone they trust listens to them, older children can talk their way through their fears, especially if they can be encouraged to go over it more than once. Encouraging a child to draw pictures of their fears can really help, especially if they are hard to describe.

It's better to try to help them talk about their worries during the daytime rather than at night when they are tired. It's also easier for them to talk if they are actively doing something with their hands at the same time – even eating a meal. Try to find the best moments to question gently, to listen and watch their faces, and to recognise hints when they are given. Accept their feelings and thoughts as real and important. Sharing a worry always helps to lift the load. Your child may then be able to sleep more soundly as a result.

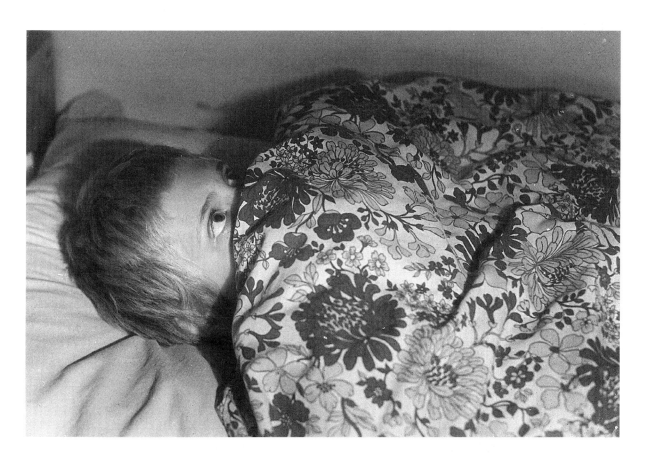

Does her diet need adjusting?

Is she eating too late in the evening, or eating foods containing additives or too much sugar? These could make her mind hyperactive and unbalance her system. If you think this is so and you would like more detailed information, the Right from the Start book *Food For Thought* will help you.

Is she getting enough exercise and natural, outdoor light during the day?

Children really do need to run and jump and cavort around, and stretch all their muscles and fill their lungs every single day. Children also need natural light from the sun to keep healthy and to feel at ease at the end of the day. So do all of us. It can be hard to plan for this in a city and in the winter time but it is worth doing all you can, as it does make a child feel more relaxed, and healthier all round.

Dawn waking

First decide on the time you think is OK for your child to get out of bed and begin the day. Give her a clock if she is old enough to tell the time. If she wakes up earlier and comes to find you, take her back to bed. Say nothing at all or just the bare minimum. For example: *It's still night time, everyone is asleep – go back to sleep.* If waking too early continues to be a problem you may want to shift her bedtime, 15 minutes at a time, over 4 or 5 days, to an hour later, so your child begins to sleep an hour later in the morning. Heavy curtains that cut out the light from early spring and summer dawns can help too.

You could also leave toys, books and a drink within reach beside her bed after she has fallen asleep the previous evening, so she finds them waiting for her in the morning.

You may decide to allow your child into your room at a particular hour to play quietly or cuddle in bed with you until you are ready to get up. Be dull and silent yourself during this time, so that the idea of fun with you doesn't stir her early out of sleeping.

Reward

Some parents reward an undisturbed night next morning with special attention or star chart stickers leading to a treat or prize. Think what might be the best way, depending on her age, interests and understanding. But most of all reward her with your pride and pleasure.

Though it works for some, the giving of a reward has one possible disadvantage. It links a good night's sleep with special behaviour that deserves reward. The question it raises is this: if we are trying to instil in our children that sleep is just a normal part of the rhythm of life, then should a peaceful night be rewarded as if it is a special deed? One way round this problem might be to tell the child that the reward is for not disturbing the rest of the household when she wakes, instead of linking it to her sleeping through the night.

Nightmares

Nightmares seem to be a part of growing up. As children become more and more aware of themselves and the world around them, anxieties about things not understood can creep in and reappear in their dream life. A nightmare can also be a sign of a child's developing conscience and his more urgent searching for understanding of what everything is about. Or a nightmare may be triggered simply by a sound, sight or remark that has disturbed the child. Many things can cause nightmares, but some of the most common include:

- Emotional struggles that have cropped up during the day
- 'Lost' feelings caused by first going to a childminder, a playgroup, school, a strange bed or anywhere unknown – or the arrival of a new baby
- Confusing or frightening television programmes or stories, or an introduction to the idea of death and dying
- Wild and exciting games just before bedtime
- Certain foods or food additives, or a too late and too fatty or sugary last meal of the day

If your child has a nightmare, and is too young to understand that it was only a dream, hold, stroke, kiss and rock her just as you would after a frightening event in the daytime. Be peaceful, not anxious, yourself. If you react too strongly, she will get the message that there is something to be worried about. Seeing that everything around her is functioning as normal will reassure a young child.

Older children need to be listened to and talked with as well as held and hugged. As they have more developed imaginations, they may need you to stay with them longer if they feel afraid to go back to sleep. They need to be told that it was a dream, that it's all over, that they are completely safe and that you are there to protect them.

An older child may need more than your words. You may need to open cupboard doors and check under the bed for her to show all is well. You can help your child to imagine a kind of 'protector' who will look after her at night. This 'protector' could be related to your idea of God, or it could be the child's special angel that watches over her, or you could use her favourite fictional characters by pinning pictures of them round her bed to look after her at night.

If your child suffers repeated nightmares, think about what might be making her anxious. Simple, comforting things can help, like leaving the door ajar to let household noise filter in; complete silence can seem eerie to children. Also try sitting with her after she has got into bed for a few, unhurried minutes of affectionate and peaceful talk before she goes to sleep. It makes a child feel safe and special in her parents' eyes to have this individual attention at the end of the day, and may reduce the likelihood of bad dreams a few hours later.

Disturbed sleep in children is often caused by nightmares triggered by TV or video characters. Dr Edelston of the Bradford Child Guidance Clinic found that half the children he examined experienced such nightmares. Few of their parents realised their children suffered bad dreams, and were shocked when they saw their children's drawings.

If your child suffers disturbed sleep, try to find out if he is having bad dreams. If so, take stock of what he is watching, and see what happens if he stops watching such programmes. One father tried this with his child – and found even the news disturbing. He tried less TV and more bedtime stories, and his son stopped having disturbed nights.

Martin Large: Set Free Childhood, *Hawthorn Press 2003*

When daytime fears cause dreams
or dreams cause daytime fears

When my child was crying in the night I used to hold him and murmur Allah! Allah! Allah! Allah! then slowly blow it across his body with my breath.

A Bangladeshi mother

If my child is scared or wakes from a bad dream I hold her, stroke her and chant a prayer to comfort her.

A Pakistani mother

If you have, yourself, some sense of God's love and protection it can really help to remind your child: Don't forget! Your own special angel is always there to keep you safe at night.

An English mother

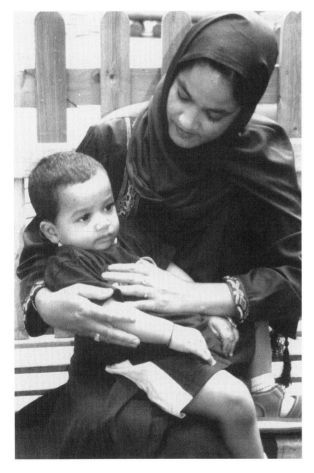 

'Daytime fears'

Sometimes there is a link between daytime fears and frightening things that crop up in dreams. A daytime fright can show up again in a dream. Occasionally, a nightmare can even lead to a daytime fear. For instance, a child may develop a sudden and completely irrational fear of an animal, insect, bird or even a noise or a place without there seeming to be any reason at all for such a panic. Research at the Children's Hospital in Boston and findings from other sleep clinics suggest that the cause of this can lie in dim memories of fright in a nightmare. These can become linked to something in the everyday world because of a faint similarity to something that once scared the child in a dream.

When we understand that this can happen, it becomes easier to see the importance of patience and reassurance, over weeks if necessary, so that a child's nightmare is not able to turn into a life-long aversion, or even a phobia. To say: *Don't be so silly – it can't hurt you! Stop fussing* can make things worse rather than better.

Whether the fear initially arose during the daytime or during a nightmare, one good way to help the jitters fade away completely is to play games that involve the child or you pretending to be the animal or insect or whatever has become the focus for her fears. Acting out a 'day in the life' of it together, inventing a family for it, giving names, describing and finding the food it needs, the sleeping place to curl up in and inventing a few friendly adventures can bring everything back to normality, even result in a special affection for the creature that had become the reason for panic.

Drawing pictures and pinning them up helps too, and, if it's possible, helping in the care of any pet, or the tidying, cleaning and decorating of a scary place. Young children love watering the soil for a tired worm, rescuing a spider with a jar and sheet of paper and putting it carefully on a wall outside. It is worth the effort to do such things, especially if the child needs this help.

Night terrors

Night terrors are very rare indeed and will probably only happen once in a child's lifetime if they ever happen at all. But we still need to be able to recognise them and know what is best to do, just in case they do come.

A night terror fills a child with wild panic while she is still deeply asleep. She screams and sits bolt upright. She may thrash about, screaming and muttering, leap out of bed and run everywhere she can, with her eyes wide open just as if she was awake, crying out for you but unable to see you. She will show all the physical symptoms of fear – a pounding heart, sweating and heaving chest. Neither your voice nor your hands wake her. This can make parents' hearts pound too!

The most frightening part of a night terror for parents is that touching her or trying to pick her up to comfort her may only increase her panic.

She cannot recognise it's you beside her, nor that it is you talking to her and touching her. Anything that touches her may seem to be the 'monster' of her dream. The best way to help is to stay with her to prevent her hurting herself, allowing the night terror to run its course and the screaming to subside.

Never shake her or shout to wake her. Try not to wake her at all. If you feel you must wake her to bring the terror to a quicker end, the best way is to hold her gently and swiftly and wipe her face with a cold, wet cloth. If she does wake, do not question her, just comfort her silently and get her quickly back into her bed. Keep as calm and matter-of-fact as you can. Do not mention what has happened the next day. It is all over and done with. If it happens again, talk to your health visitor for reassurance.

Babara Kahan, an expert on childcare, describes a child's needs at night

A child's sleeping place needs to be safe, warm, comfortable and familiar with a cuddly toy, perhaps a special blanket or small pillow – and a loved and comforting adult within reach.

Sleeping away from home in a strange bed and strange room can make some children miserable and tense.

Every child should be restored and developed a little each 24 hours through sleep. This can't happen if the hours of darkness are peopled by bad dreams and tension. We need to watch out for this and understand why, so we can think out ways to lay the anxiety to rest at such times for them.

Peace pictures in the mind

If your older child finds it hard to get to sleep, or can't get back to sleep in the night, you can help her by telling her a picture story that is like a happy dream in itself. In this way, the chatter of her wide-awake mind can grow still, and peaceful feelings can fill her instead. Seeing beautiful and soothing pictures of a special place with our mind's eye, and actually being in that place in our imagination, can be a big comfort. Being left in that place in our imagination to play, with no more words said, becomes a gentle magic that can tip a tired child into sleep in no time at all.

Decide on the place you are going to 'paint' for her and think of each of the details you are going to describe. But you will need to start with some idea of what she would love. You will need to have all the ideas ready in your head before you begin. What will there be in that beautiful garden or the other special place you have chosen to explore? What will you describe? A stream, a waterfall, shining pebbles, a pond, a pool surrounded by moss and yellow flowers, two kittens playing in the long grass, waves chasing each other across the wet sand by the

sea, a bright blue swing hanging from a gigantic pine tree, a hillside covered in flowers with a path leading to somewhere, a house hidden up a tree; a bird calling *Follow me!*

As well as describing these things, you will need to involve your child during the dream-story, so she is drawn into the adventure and not left just looking at everything you describe to her. She needs to start to play with it all, so it's important to say things like …

Open the gate now and walk into your special garden.

Take off your shoes if you like and paddle through the stream. Watch the sparkling water dancing over the stones. Feel it tickling your bare feet.

Run, climb up the ladder. Up, up you go through the green leaves till you reach your tree house hidden in the branches. Open the wooden door. Now you can see what's inside.

It is important that you leave her playing, uninterrupted, in the place you have taken her to, with what you have shown her … in her garden, on the hillside, in the tree house, with the kittens or with the beautiful stones. From there, her own imagination will carry her until she slips into sleep.

If the child is particularly tense, or finds it difficult to enter into a dream-story, there are some suggestions you can make before you start. These are only ideas but you can adapt them as you choose:

1 Begin always by telling your child: *Close your eyes.*
2 Then, before you even start leading her mind to a special place, concentrate on a star in the sky. For example say: *Look up into the sky and see the dark blue velvetiness and the stars shining everywhere. Imagine there is one star in the sky that belongs just to you. Find it! It is your own special star shining down on you now. Its light is shining on your hair and your face and running all over your arms and hands right to your fingertips. Every part of you now is full of silvery light and this makes you feel warm and happy and ready to enjoy what is coming next.*
3 The next important job to do is to help her get rid of any worries jumping about in her head. You can do this by saying something like this: *Now we are going to go to your own special garden (or beautiful mountain or magic park or whatever you have thought of) but, before we go through the gate, look at the little, green bush growing beside it. That bush is called the Worry Bush. Any worries you have got in your head, anything at all, you can hang on the Worry Bush. It will take all your worries away from you. So, stop for a moment and do a little hanging on the bush if you want to. (Pause) Now you can open the gate and walk through it into your own garden.* You can invent other objects to hold her worries, like a dustbin or a box.

Tips for the storyteller

- Use a slow, relaxed, quiet voice while you are talking
- Leave long enough pauses for her to imagine doing what you suggest.

If you find you have enjoyed painting peace pictures for your child in this way, you might find another Right from the Start book valuable. It is called *Stillness, Imagination and Meditation for Children.*

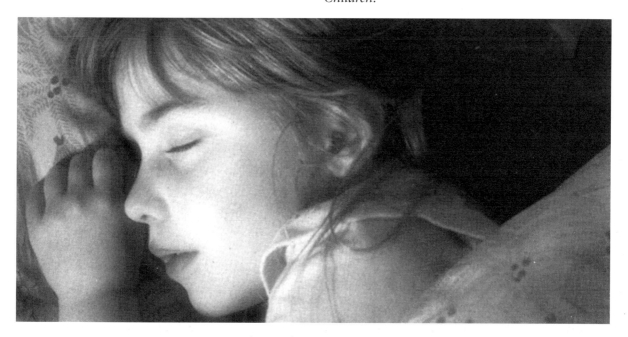

'First close your eyes'

I can hear all my cries and laughter at once.
I can hear that my joy and pain are one.

Thich Nhat Hanh

In a nutshell

- Older children will have bedtime ups and downs, just as they did when they were babies and toddlers.
- Happy associations with bed are important.
- Bedtime routine may need adjusting to fit your child's age and energy level. Try arranging a wind-down activity for her to do alone in her bed until she feels sleepy. Try changing the routine if it has become stale or needs adjusting as the child grows older.
- Bedtime routines can be disrupted by a new baby in the family, working hours and other pressures on you. It is worth every effort to restore the routine.

- Search for a wider cause if there are still problems.
- Give encouragement and reward your child.
- Nightmares can be caused by a number of things including emotional struggles, a change in routine, confusion, fear, over-excitement, and even diet. These should be explored.
- Night terrors are very rare indeed and will probably only happen once in a child's lifetime if they ever happen at all.
- If your older child finds it hard to get to sleep, or can't get back to sleep in the night, you can help her by telling her a picture story.

CHAPTER 9

From Surviving to Thriving

When a child is sleeping through the night, and everyone in the family is getting the rest they need, the whole world changes colour. You can finally enjoy watching your sleeping baby or toddler without the sinking feeling of wondering how long the peace will last. You can begin thinking about all you might do with your child, and the pleasure of his company – even at bedtime. You are no longer just surviving, you are THRIVING!

Spirit and soul

When we are happy and rested, evening and early morning are often times of soft and shining joy between parents and their young children. It may be dark outside; the busy-ness of the day is over, or has not yet begun. There is time for tenderness, with no interruption.

After what we have been through, it's just amazing to get a whole night's sleep most nights each week!

Alex

Not being jerked awake again and again each night – I can't believe it!

Sara

I used to creep into bed with such a sense of dread of what would happen during the next few hours – now I never give it a thought.

Sam

My husband and I had come to feel so angry with each other all the time. I thought it must be my fault that the baby cried so much. I must be to blame. Now it's like love coming back into our lives.

Veronica

It's so wonderful to be able to say to Ben, 'Goodnight, see you in the morning!'

Beth

Suddenly, after all this, it's like a flood of relief and amazement when I wake up each morning. I'd forgotten what it felt like to laugh…and to hear myself talking about next week. It's seemed like a half-life forever but now I can breathe again, think again and love my whole family again. My baby is brilliant…and now I begin to think I am too!

Elaine

Recovery and Healing

If evenings had become a time of struggle and dread for you and it has been a long, tough journey discovering ways to calm your child when he's very distressed – you may need to make a real effort to bring beauty back to bedtime.

Sharing some peaceful time together just before he sleeps is the best way to do this – there should be no interruptions if possible. Try speaking, chanting or singing a verse, a rhyme or a prayer together, looking at beautiful pictures or

Suddenly, as I held my newborn child in the darkness, I felt my soul jump up with the wonder of it all. It was like a flame inside me!

Seguna

I can remember feeling so close to the whole world and so full of hope - lying at night with my baby in my arms!

Emma

family photographs. Then perhaps singing a lullaby or gentle song which will be like a warm blanket around him as he slips towards sleep. These shared times are truly food for the soul.

For books, tapes and CDs of music to share with your child see the Music, Riddles and Rhymes section at the end of this book. The Right from the Start book called *Beginning with Singing* may also give you some good ideas.

Following are some examples of a few simple verses, prayers and lullabies which you might enjoy together at the end of the day.

Verses and Prayers

Four corners to my bed,
Four angels round my head.
One to watch and two to pray,
And one to keep all fear away.

Jenny Dent

The Lord bless you and keep you:
The Lord make his face to shine upon you,
And be gracious to you:
The Lord lift up his countenance upon you,
and give you peace.

The Bible, *Numbers 6:24–26*

Now I lay me down to sleep.
I pray Thee, Lord, my soul to keep.
Your love be with me through the night
And wake me with the morning light.

Traditional

Peace to you from my heart to your heart.

Sufi

> My 3-year-old caught every bug around and in the winter was struggling against illness and the misery of being on antibiotics most of the time. I often used to sing *God be in my head* to him just as I settled him for the night. After a bit, he wouldn't go to sleep without it and I ended up having to sing it every night for over a year, in spite of the fact that I never got the tune quite right.
>
> *Sarah*

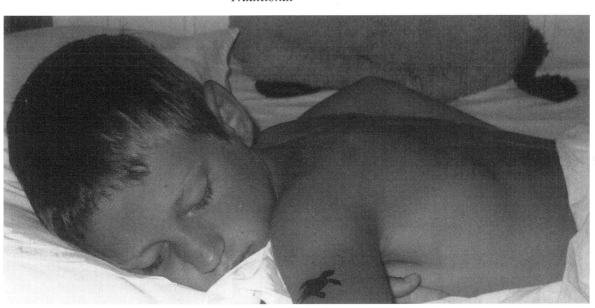

God of all our cities,
Each alley, street, and square,
Pray look down on every house
And bless the people there.

*   *   *

I bind unto myself today
The power of God to hold and lead,
His eye to watch, his might to stay,
His ear to hearken to my need

The wisdom of my God to teach,
His hand to guide, his shield to ward;
The word of God to give me speech,
His heavenly host to be my guard.

God bless all those that I love;
God bless all those that love me;
God bless all those that love those that I love
And all those that love those that love me.

*   *   *

Lord, keep us safe this night,
Secure from all our fear.
May angels guard us while we sleep,
Till morning light appears.

*   *   *

God be in my head, and in my understanding:
God be in mine eyes, and in my looking:
God be in my mouth and in my speaking;
God be in my heart, and in my thinking;
God be at my end, and at my departing.

from a Book of Hours

Lullabies
Hush-a-baw birdie

Hush-a-baw birdie, croon, croon,
Hush-a-baw birdie, croon,
The sheep are gane to silver wood,
And the cows are gane to the broom, broom,

Chorus   And it's braw milking the kye, kye,
And it's braw milking the kye,
The birds are singing, the bells are ringing,

The wild deer come galloping by, by.

And hush-a-baw birdie, croon, croon,
Hush-a-baw birdie, croon,
The gaits are gane to the mountain high,
And they'll be no hame till noon, noon.

Chorus

Hush little baby

Hush little baby, don't say a word,
Mamma's going to buy you a mockingbird.
If that mockingbird won't sing,
Mamma's going to buy you a diamond ring.
If that diamond ring turns brass,
Mamma's going to buy you a looking glass.
If that looking glass gets broke,
Mamma's going to buy you a billy goat.

If that billy goat won't pull,
Mamma's going to buy you a cart and bull.
If that cart and bull turn over,
Mamma's going to buy you a dog named Rover.
If that dog named Rover don't bark,
Mamma's going to buy you a horse and cart.
If that horse and cart fall down,
You'll still be the prettiest baby in town.

Golden Slumbers

Golden Slumbers kiss your eyes,
Smiles awake you when you rise.
Sleep pretty darling do not cry,
And I will sing a lullaby.
Lullaby, lullaby, lullaby.

Care you know not, therefore sleep,
While I o'er you watch do keep.
Sleep pretty darling do not cry,
And I will sing a lullaby.
Lullaby, lullaby, lullaby.

The riddle song

Moderato

I gave my love a cherry that has no stone,
I gave my love a chicken that has no bone,
I gave my love a ring that has no end,
I gave my love a baby that's no crying.

How can there be a cherry that has no stone?
How can there be a chicken that has no bones?

How can there be a ring that has no end?
How can there be a baby that's no crying?

A cherry when it's blooming it has no stone,
A chicken when it's pipping it has no bone,
A ring when it's rolling it has no end,
A baby when it's sleeping there's no crying.

Hush-a- bye

Hush-a-bye, don't you cry
Go to sleep little baby.
When you wake, you shall have cake
And all the pretty little horses

Coach and six white horses
All the pretty little horses.

La la sana

La la sana la la
Wey'm shel wane

Ksa sa umgabele
Wey'm shel wane

Bye Baby Bunting

Bye Baby Bunting
Daddy's gone a-hunting,
To get a little rabbit skin
To wrap poor Baby Bunting in.
Bye, Baby Bunting.

Swaddling

What is swaddling?

Swaddling is the art of wrapping a baby snugly in a sheet or light blanket so that it gives her the same feeling of warmth and security as being back in the womb. **It is designed for newborn babies up to four weeks old only**.

What are the risks?

- There is research evidence (Ref. *Birth to 5*, 2000 p. 20–1) to suggest that swaddling may lead to overheating, which is a cot death risk factor. For this reason some midwives and health visitors do not encourage swaddling.
- After 4 weeks old, swaddling, because it reduces movement, can restrict the development of a baby's muscles.

What are the benefits?

- The baby can enjoy the familiar, peaceful sensation she felt when in the womb. During her first few weeks of life, it may be comforting for her to feel 'cocooned' again, and can help prevent her flailing her arms, scratching herself, or becoming startled by her own reflexes.

How to swaddle

- Spread a soft sheet or baby blanket on a flat surface and fold down the top edge.
- Lay the baby towards one side of the blanket, with her head just above the folded edge. Gently hold her arms down across her chest with one hand, while you lift the shorter bit of the blanket, taking it across her chest and tucking it under her shoulder. Now lift the other side of the blanket, pull it towards you across her chest and tuck it firmly right round under her back so she is like a little sausage-shaped parcel. You will have to roll her over for a moment to do this smoothly.
- Some babies love being swaddled sometimes, others never. See how she reacts each time you do it – she will soon show you what she feels. She knows best!
- Be careful not to swaddle too tightly and don't leave her alone when she is swaddled up or for too long at a time. Loosen the blanket a little later so she can get her fists up to her mouth when she wants to.

Tips to remember

- It is sensible to avoid swaddling your baby in a very warm room unless you use a very thin cotton sheet to do so.
- If you are concerned about overheating and decide not to swaddle, carrying your baby in a sling-type carrier is another way to help her feel safe and secure.

Cot death

'Cot death' or 'sudden infant death syndrome' (SIDS) is when an apparently healthy baby dies suddenly for no apparent reason. Research has shown that the following factors are known to increase the risk of cot death.

- smoking
- if the baby becomes too hot

Reducing the risk

There are nine key steps parents and carers should take to reduce the risk of cot death:

- Cut smoking in pregnancy – fathers too!

- Do not let anyone smoke in the same room as your baby.

- Settle the baby to sleep on her back. This position will not increase the risk of choking.

- Do not let your baby get too hot.

- Keep baby's head uncovered – place your baby with their feet to the end of the cot, to prevent wriggling down under the covers.

- Keep your baby close to you for the first six months.

- It's dangerous to share a bed with your baby if you or your partner
  - are smokers (no matter where or when you smoke),
  - have been drinking alcohol,
  - take medication or drugs that make you drowsy,
  - feel very tired.

- It's dangerous to sleep together on a sofa, armchair or settee.

- If your baby is unwell, seek medical advice promptly.

Avoiding accidents

- Avoid plastic sheets, cot bumpers, and ribbons or ties on clothing.

- Avoid loose bedding and furry toys around your baby's face.

- Don't leave the baby alone if she is swaddled, or if she is propped up on cushions on a sofa or armchair.

- Avoid the use of hot water bottles and electric blankets.

Post-natal depression

Post-natal depression affects between 10 – 15% of mothers. It is characterised by a depressed mood which overwhelms most positive feelings and may be a continuation of "baby blues".

"Baby blues" affects most mothers and is associated with tearfulness and a feeling of anticlimax after the excitement and tension of birth. This is not the same as post-natal depression.

How to recognise it

Many of the symptoms of depression are similar to normal feelings after having a baby, such as tiredness and lack of interest in things you normally enjoy. Mothers with depression will experience feelings of despair and hopelessness for no apparent reason. They may find it hard to concentrate and experience anxiety and panic attacks. These symptoms are more than just the 'baby blues'.

What helps

- talking to someone you trust
- Health Visitors have been specially trained to help women identify they are depressed and decide what will be most helpful and supportive
- look after yourself. Remember to eat, and rest when you can. Take help when it is offered, or ask for help
- don't be afraid to talk to your doctor. Post-natal depression is time-limited and you will recover
- the support of other women, whether or not they have experienced depression, is very valuable. Ask about support groups or post-natal groups in your area.

Ref. *Feelings after Birth*
Heather Welford, NCT 2002

Help, Support and Useful Addresses

Listed here are suggestions about what else you might do to get advice and information; where you might go to meet others in the same situation and find more friendship and support. Also listed are organisations you might join, how to find out about local branches, local initiatives and events, as well as equipment that might be useful.

National and voluntary organisations and helplines

Community Practitioners and Health Visitors Association (PHVA)

40 Bermondsey Street. London SE1 3UD
Tel: 020 7939 7000

Cry-sis

BM Cry-sis. London WC1N 3XX
Helpline: 020 7404 5011
8am – 11pm seven days a week. A central telephone referral service puts you in touch with your local telephone volunteer.
A self-help support organisation offering counselling and advice for families with sleepless and demanding babies, and providing local support groups, newsletters and publications.

Family Caring Trust

8 Ashtree Enterprise Park, Newry, Co. Down BT34 1BY
Tel: 028 3026 4174
www.familycaring.co.uk
The Trust's parenting courses – babies to teenagers – and resources, have been the very popular in Britain for the past fifteen years. Visit their website for support and further details.

Foresight

28 The Paddock. Godalming. Surrey GU7 1XD
Tel: 01483 427839
Helping prospective parents take all possible steps to ensure their baby is born physically and emotionally strong and healthy through knowing the essential facts about nutrition, pollution and the effect of smoking, alcohol and other stresses on an unborn and newborn baby. Offers help, advice and publications.

The Foundation for the Study of Infant Death (FSID)

Artillery House, 11–19 Artillery Row, London SW1P 1RT
Tel: 0870 787 0885
Helpline: 0870 787 0554
Aims to promote infant health and prevent sudden unexpected deaths in infancy. Supports bereaved families. Funds research and provides information.

Gingerbread

1st Floor, 7 Sovereign Close, Sovereign Court, London E1
Freephone Advice Telephone: 0800 018 4318
www.gingerbread.org.uk
Offers support, advice and friendship to lone parents and a network of local support groups.

HomeStart UK

2 Salisbury Road. Leicester. LE1 7QR
Tel: 0116 233 9955
Volunteers offer support, friendship and practical help to young families in their own homes. Telephone to learn more and to be put in touch with your local HomeStart scheme.

Hyperactive Children's Support Group (HACSG)

71 Whyke Lane, Chichester, W. Sussex PO19 2LD
Written enquiries only. If you think your baby's sleep problems might be caused by diet, send a SAE for information.

The Institute for Complementary Medicine

The Information Officer, P.O. Box 194, London SE16 1QZ
Send a SAE and two loose second-class stamps to cover the cost for a local address list of practitioners in other disciplines e.g. herbal medicine, allergy therapy, nutritional therapy.

International Association of Infant Massage (IAIM)

Their website gives details of local people trained in infant massage.

La Leche League. GB.

BM3424. London WC1N 3XX
Tel: 020 7242 1278
Telephone counselling, mother-to-mother support groups, breastfeeding help and information.

Meet a Mum Association (MAMA)

Helpline: 020 8768 0123 (Monday to Friday 7–10pm)
Mama organises local groups offering support to mothers who feel isolated or who may be suffering from post-natal depression.

National Childbirth Trust

Alexandra House, Oldham Terrace, Acton, London W3 6NH
Tel: 020 8992 8637
N.C.T. Enquiries: 08704 448707
Provides support in pregnancy, childbirth and early parenthood. Breastfeeding help and encouragement. Co-ordinates local support groups.

Newpin

Sutherland House. 35 Sutherland Square. Walworth. London SE17 3EE
Tel: 020 7703 6326
Helping parents under stress. Runs 16 Newpin Centres, a Fathers and Families project, and a Young Mums project which gives support in particular to mothers who are lonely and discouraged, suffer from post-natal depression, have difficulties coping or who feel violent towards their babies and young children.

NSPCC

42 Curtain Road, London EC2A 3NH
Helpline: 0808 800 5000
Other languages:
Welsh: 0808 100 2524
(free 24 hours a day service)
Bengali: 0800 096 7714
Gujarati: 0800 096 7715
Hindi: 0800 096 7716
Punjabi: 0800 096 7717
Urdu: 0800 096 7718 (Open 11am – 7pm)
Provides counselling, information and advice to anyone worried about a child at risk of abuse. The NSPCC also publishes a range of free parenting book-lets for example Handle With Care, *on how to hold and look after your baby, including advice on how to cope with persistent crying. Also:* Stress: A guide for parents, *helping you to identify and manage stress.*

Osteopathic Centre for Children

109 Harley Street, London W1N 1DG
Tel: 020 7486 6160
Provides a checking service and the gentle manipulation sometimes needed to realign the bones of a baby's or young child's skull displaced during the pressures of birth.

The Osteopathic Information Service

P.O. Box 2074, Reading, Berkshire RG1 4YR
Tel: 020 7799 2559 (Monday to Friday 9am–5pm)
Send SAE for details of local cranial osteopaths working with babies and young children.
Two other telephone numbers may be able to help you as well:
The Sutherland Society, (Cranial Osteopaths) Enquiry Line: 0845 6030680
The General Osteopathic Council 020 7357 6655 or 6242

Parentline Plus

520 Highgate Studios, 53-59 Highgate Road, Kentish Town, London NW5 1TL
Tel: 020 7284 5500
Helpline: 0808 800 2222
E-mail: centraloffice@parentlineplus.org.uk
www.parentlineplus.org.uk
The national network of helplines for parents under stress. Runs courses on parenting skills. Ask for more details and to find a course near you.

Positive Parenting

2A South Street, Gosport, PO12 1ES
Tel: 023 9252 8787
Publishes a Positive Parenting pack and runs a confidence-building course for parents of 0–7 year olds called 'Time Out for Parents'. There may be a course within reach of you or a parent group using the Positive Parenting Manual or the Time Out for Parents workbook.

Association for Post-natal Illness

Tel: 020 7386 0868
Offers one-to-one support to mothers suffering from post-natal-illness.

Relate

To find your local branch look under Relate in your telephone directory (England, Wales and Northern Ireland) or under Couple Counselling (Scotland).
A confidential counselling service for anyone with relationship problems.

Society for the Promotion of Nutritional Therapy

P.O. Box 47, Heathfield, East Sussex TN21 8ZX.
Send £1 (in stamps or a coin attached to a card) for a list of qualified nutritional practitioners (not medical practitioners) if you are concerned about food allergy or nutritional deficiency.

The British Homeopathic Association

27A Devonshire Street, London W1N 1RJ
Tel: 020 7935 2163
Homeopathic treatment can often help a distressed, sleepless, crying child.
Send a SAE for a list of doctors trained in homeopathy, an information pack and availability of N.H.S. treatment.

The British Society for Allergy, Environmental and Nutritional Medicine

P.O. Box 28, Totton, Southampton SO40 2ZA
Tel: 01703 813912
Do not contact this organisation directly but ask your GP to contact them in order to refer you to a private registered medical practitioner specialising in food/ chemical allergy, intolerance and nutrition.

The BSD Earth Energies Group

C/o Mr A Riggs, Head of Science and Technology, 33 Parvills, Parklands Estate, Waltham Abbey, Essex EN9 1QG
If you are concerned about earth or man-made radiation affecting your child's sleeping place and would like to ask a professional to measure the levels, send an SAE with your request.

Association of Child Psychotherapists

120 Westheath Road, London NW3 7TU
Tel: 020 8458 1609

Child Psychotherapy Trust

Star House, 104–108 Grafton Road, London NW5 4BD
Tel: 020 8284 1355
If you think you need experienced help of this kind for your child, contact one of these organisations, ask for advice and the name of a registered child psychotherapist near you. Then ask your GP to refer you. Child psychotherapists are available privately and through the N.H.S

Useful books

Angela Henderson, *The Good Sleep Guide for You and Your Baby*

Hawthorn Press, Stroud, 2003
A step by step guide to the prevention and cure of sleep problems from birth to 18 months. Easy-to-use questionnaire format with pull-out sleep diary. It also contains a useful appendix on how to wean your baby off night feeds.

Eileen Hayes, *Crying*

Pan Books, London, 1999.

The following four helpful books are distributed by the National Childbirth Trust:

Anna McGrail, *Crying Baby*

Thorsons and N.C.T., London, 1998.
About the difficulties of identifying the causes of a new baby's crying, how to recognise the sounds and what they mean, how to respond to the child's individual personality. Highly recommended.

Penney Hames, *The Book of Sleep*

Thorsons and N.C.T., London, 1998.
Gives background information and offers practical steps to help you establish a routine and look after your own needs as well as the needs of your child.

Sheila Kitzinger, *The Year After Childbirth*

Oxford University Press, Oxford, 1994.
Practical suggestions to help new mothers through the physical and emotional changes that usually occur during the first, often turbulent, year of caring for a baby.

N.C.T., *Early Days – What it's really like to have a new baby*

National Childbirth Trust, 2002.
Booklet giving an account in parents' own words, of what to expect in the first few weeks.

To order any of the four books listed above, contact: N.C.T Maternity Sales, 239 Shawbridge Street, Glasgow G43 1QN
Telephone: 0141 636 0600 www.nctms.co.uk

Lynne Murray and Liz Andrews, *The Social Baby: Understanding Babies' Communication from Birth*
The Children's Project Ltd, Richmond, 2000
A ground-breaking book showing how babies actively communicate from the moment of birth, and how to interpret their behaviour as a language of communication. Covering sociability, crying and sleep problems from birth to four months. Over 700 colour photographs.

Helen and Clive Dorman, *The Social Toddler: Promoting Positive Behaviour*
The Children's Project Ltd, Richmond, 2002
This book brings the minds of children to life and provides valuable insights into all aspects of children's behaviour. It covers the mental development of children from 12 months to 4 years. Over 1700 colour pictures.

Babycheck
ISBN 0–9525227–0–5.
Developed by a team of paediatricians in Cambridge, this booklet gives you 19 checkpoints and a chart to help you discover whether or not your baby is ill.
Order from P.O. Box 324. Wroxham. Norwich. Norfolk NR12 8EQ

Elizabeth Hayden, *Osteopathy for Children*
Gloucester, 2000.
This book explains clearly and simply how osteopathy can be of benefit to babies and children, and mothers during and after pregnancy.
Order from: Churchdown Osteopaths, 102 Chosen Drive, Churchdown, Gloucester GL3 2QU (Tel. 01452 714511)

Deborah Jackson, *Three in a Bed. Why you should sleep with your baby*
Bloomsbury, London, 1989.
A practical guide and full of medical and historical evidence about the benefits of sleeping with your baby. Looks at all the problems and challenges in depth and from a wide range of perspectives.

Francoise Freedman *Baby Yoga – gentle exercises for babies, mums and dads*
Gaia Books Ltd., London, 2000.
Parenting skills learnt from the Amazon Forest people inspired this book. It describes the art of handling babies with great confidence, physically playing with them instead of just jigging them up and down, and nourishing and relaxing them through shared, especially adapted yoga movement and touch. The author believes that this experience lays a foundation for non-violence and well-being throughout life.
Available from Touch-Needs Ltd, Unit 3, Elm Farm Industrial Park, Bramshall, Uttoxeter, Staffs ST14 5BE

Vimala McClure, *Infant Massage: A Handbook for Loving Parents*
Bantam Books, New York, 2000.
Vimala set up the International Association of Infant Massage and worked in one of Mother Theresa's baby hospitals in India.
Available from Touch-Needs Ltd, Unit 3, Elm Farm Industrial Park, Bramshall, Uttoxeter, Staffs ST14 5BE

Peter Walker, *Baby Massage*
Piatkus Books, Grantham, 1998.

Maria Mercati, *Tui Na Massage for a healthier, brighter child*
Gaia Books, London, 1999.
Traditional Chinese massage techniques of kneading, squeezing and rubbing. Includes massage treatment for night crying and restlessness, colic and teething.

Jean Liedloff, *The Continuum Concept*
Penguin, London, 1989.
A passionate plea to Western parents to keep in closer touch with their babies for the first nine months (after experiencing life with the Yequana Indians in Venezuela for two and a half years and seeing the contentment and competence of their children).

Dr. Richard Ferber,
Solve Your Child's Sleep Problems.
The Complete Practical Guide for Parents
Dorling Kindersley, London, 1992.
Draws on seven years of research into infant sleep and sleep disorders at the Centre for Pediatric Sleep Disorders at the Children's Hospital in Boston. The author describes the hundreds of families he has treated, the different approaches he has used, and the bad advice so often given to parents which only makes matters worse.

Julian Scott, *Natural Medicine for Children*
Unwin Hyman, London, 1990.

Martin Large, *Set Free Childhood*
Hawthorn Press, Stroud, 2003.

Robert Munsch, *Love You Forever*
Firefly Books Ltd, Bellevue, USA, 1986.
A beautiful and simple picture book about the enduring and unconditional love a parent has for a child from the day they are born and throughout their lives. A book to share with your children and anyone you love (age 2–7).

Regina J. Williams, *What if …*
Illumination Arts, Bellevue, USA, 2001.
If you have children who are ever reluctant to go to bed, they will love this book! What If … *features a little boy who uses his fantastic imagination to delay bedtime for as long as possible. Reading this enchanting, dream-inspiring story will make bedtime fun (age 3–7).*

H. Elizabeth Collins, *To Sleep with the Angels*
Illumination Arts, Bellevue, USA, 2001.
This beautiful lyrical, gentle tale inspires children to explore their potential to be what they want to be and to live their dreams (age 3–8).

To order *Love You Forever, What if …* and *To Sleep with the Angels* contact:

Words of Discovery,
FREEPOST LON7858, Leicester, LE5 6ZY
Tel: 0845 458 1199
Website: www.wordsofdiscovery.com

Music, Riddles and Rhymes

Books

Candy Verney, *The Singing Day*
Hawthorn Press, Stroud, Autumn 2003.
Book and CD
An excellent introduction to singing with your child from the very beginning, including ways of overcoming your own difficulties with singing. Emphasis on the rhythms and routines of the day.

Candy Verney, *The Singing Year*
Hawthorn Press, Stroud, Autumn 2003.
Book and CD
A companion volume to 'The Singing Day' with emphasis on the rhythms, routines and festivals of the seasonal round.

Opal Dunn, *Hippety-Hop Hippety-Hay*
Frances Lincoln Publishers, Colchester 2001.
A selection of interactive rhymes for young babies to three-year-olds graded for use according to age.

Brien Masters, *The Waldorf Song Book*
Floris Books, Edinburgh, 1997.

CDs

Baby Songs
A CD of gentle nursery rhymes and lullabies to listen to and sing to your baby.

Ami Tomake
A CD of a Bengali chant from India which means 'I love you my dear baby'. Its

wonderfully soothing effect on babies has made it a favourite in infant massage classes.

Sleepy Time Playsongs

Restful songs, rhymes and lullabies for relaxed play and soothing bedtimes. Suitable for babies and children from birth to 3 years.

Music for Dreaming

Performed by the Melbourne Symphony Orchestra. A CD of continuous music which has been produced to bring balance and harmony to the mind and body. The traditional instruments used, flute, harp and strings have a natural harmonic quality that resonate within our body, bringing a sense of pleasure and peace to tired parents!

All four CDs and Sleepy Time Playsongs can be obtained from Touch Needs Ltd. See list of suppliers below.

The following 3 CDs can be ordered from Musikgarten (see below)
Music for Dancing & Playing CD
Music for Movement & Stories CD
Sounds of Nature (including set of 32 picture cards) CD

Organisation

Musikgarten UK, Chapel House, Bow, Crediton, Devon EX17 6HN
(Tel/fax: 01363 82913)
Musikgarten specialises in music and movement for parents and young children. They also provide musical development training for nursery schools and pre-school groups and supply quality instruments and CDs.

Suppliers

The Nutri Centre

7 Park Crescent, London W1B 1PF
Website: www.nutricentre.com
The Nutri Centre is Europe's leading centre for complementary medicine. They can supply every nutritional remedy you might need for yourself or your child and they also offer professional advice. For orders and advice telephone 020 9436 5122 or email enq@nutricentre.com. There is also an extensive library and bookshop in the Education Resource Centre. For book orders and library services telephone 020 7636 0276.

Britannia Health Products Ltd

41–51 Brighton Road, Redhill, Surrey RH1 6YS
Tel: 01737 773741 Website: www.colief.com

Britannia Health Products is the UK distributor for 'Colief', the new remedy for colic. To find out more, visit the Colief website.

The Trafford NHS Healthcare Trust

The Delamere Centre, Delamere Avenue, Stretford, Manchester M32 0DF   Tel: 0161 864 0329
'Sweet Dreams' 15 minute video. Aims at solving sleep problems in the pre-school child.

Touch Needs Ltd

Unit 3, Elm Farm Industrial Park, Bramshall, Uttoxeter, Staffordshire ST14 5BE
Tel: 01889 560260 Website: www.touchneeds.com
This company supplies CDs of calming music and songs for babies and young children. It also sells a wide range of books on infant care, touch and massage for professionals and parents, massage practice dolls and massage oils.

John Lewis Stores

Oxford Street, London W1   Tel: 020 7629 7711
Supply a swinging cradle for babies from birth to four months, and also a car seat which is also a three-speed baby rocker which you set to rock for 15 minutes at a time.

The Right from the Start 'BedNest'

Priory Holdings, Kington St Michael,
nr Chippenham, Wiltshire SN14 6JR.
Tel: 01249 750208
Email: cillalab@aol.com
This light, neat, fold-up bedside cot was specially designed for Right from the Start. It is an inexpensive and simple solution for mothers who want to keep their under-7-month-old babies in close touch all night. It has telescopic legs and will fix securely against beds of various heights or it can be used free-standing. It doubles as a lightweight travel cot. For illustrated details and price of the BedNest contact Priory Holdings.

Cosatto Sales Ltd

Wollaston Way, Basildon, Essex SS13 1LL
Tel: 01268 722800
Website: www.cosatto.com
Discover from this supplier the wide range of full-size cots including the Chantelle with a four-position mattress base that can be adjusted as your baby grows. This also enables the cot to be used as an extension to the parents' bed with the dropside slid under the mattress base.

Look Locally

Baby clinics and GP surgeries – *many have notice boards advertising local baby and toddler groups.* Community midwives, nurses and health visitors – *can offer practical help and ideas for getting in touch with other parents.*

One O'clock Clubs and other baby and toddler groups – *find out about them via your Local Authority.* Local libraries – *keep lists of local associations and have notice boards where clubs and events are advertised.*

Friends and Family

Use the telephone.
If you can't easily get out, ask people to come and visit you.

What is **Right from the Start**?

> The world will not change and there will be no peace if there is not a new education.
> *U. Thant, former Secretary General to the United Nations*

This vision grew into an international human rights education project called **Right from the Start**. This aims to help parents expand their knowledge and explore new ideas, approaches and parenting skills. It also believes that parents deserve greater opportunities to share valuable experiences with each other. Together, parents can become part of a strong community that will support both themselves and their children. **Right from the Start** believes this sharing and strength within the community is the key to reducing violence in society. It presents a wide-ranging, integrated series of books to support and help parents and teachers.

The project is based on research and collaboration with many distinguished contributors from the UK and other countries: educationalists, child specialists and child carers and, most importantly, parents and grandparents.

Human rights education for young children means first and foremost the establishing of good human relationships. The project therefore focuses on ways of strengthening a child's experience of love, trust and security on which such qualities as compassion and justice depend.

Right from the Start aims to:

- foster and strengthen good human relationships, especially the relationship between children and adults
- bring out the inborn trust, generosity and creativity of every child so that respect and love for others can grow from this sense of self-worth
- encourage fuller recognition of the spiritual nature of every child and bring a better balance of mind, body and spirit

- bring children closer to the natural world and an understanding and care of the environment
- help to heal the harm that children can suffer in their earlier years
- help to prevent children from being drawn into a culture of violence

This book is part of a series which aims to help parents and teachers find ways of giving children:

- the attention and care they need
- loving interaction and imaginative sharing of daily life
- protection and nurturing of their 'inner life'
- time and space to be themselves
- a voice which is heard

These books also aim to support the often overwhelming tasks of parents, carers and teachers by giving them:

- fresh new ideas – as well as reminders of some old ones
- creative and practical opportunities to change attitudes and patterns of response
- support in bringing up children in ways that develop self-esteem, imagination, self-discipline and compassion
- a forum where they can learn from each other, and help build community

The **Right from the Start** dolphin and child logo comes from the 18ft bronze sculpture by David Wynne on London's Albert Embankment, overlooking the River Thames. It has been chosen because a dolphin has a high level of emotional intelligence, a close affinity with human beings and a special instinct and power to heal and comfort. A dolphin also has a great sense of fun.

The picture of a child and dolphin playing together symbolises the trust, affection, adventure and sense of unity in all creation which each of us should be able to experience and enjoy from earliest childhood to the end of our lives.

Peace is being without crime and violence and hating.
It is love that is passed on from generation to generation.

Clifford aged 8

Forthcoming **Right from the Start** Publications

The Right from the Start Handbook

(for teachers and teachers in training)

Introduces the whole project and presents a wide range of successful approaches and inspirational initiatives in the support of children's spiritual and mental well-being. Includes ideas and strategies for a closer partnership between teachers and parents in response to growing stresses in young children.

A Right and Gentle Beginning

Understanding the sensitivity, intelligence and memory in unborn and newborn babies and how we can respond to this in the way we welcome, calm and care for them in the first months.

Playing for Life. *Protecting children from hurtful influences and violence*

A child's need to play, in different ways, from birth onwards. The encouragement that parents can give to help a child learn to concentrate, cope well with difficulties and grow up rich in imagination, optimism and understanding.

Calmer, Easier, Happier Parenting.
Less Trouble, Blame and Punishment

Children behave well when they feel right. Helping them to feel right, to be open and honest and to make amends. Forgiving ourselves and each other. Setting boundaries and helping children's confidence and self discipline.

Let's Have a Go! *Sharing everyday skills with your child*

Bringing out children's capability, kindness and sense of self-worth.

Beginning with Singing.
The power of music to help your child

(for teachers as well as parents)

The bond that singing brings to families, schools and communities. The reduction in stress and anti-social behaviour in children through singing together. How music can heal and calm, and how it helps with other kinds of learning.

Food for Thought.
What children eat and its effect on their intelligence, personality and behaviour.

(for teachers as well as parents)

The nutrients that may be missing and the pollutants that may be absorbed. The damage that can be done to children's sensitive – because still growing – brains. Understanding the facts and finding ways to protect our children.

Natural Wonder.
The enchantment that feeds the human spirit

(for teachers as well as parents)

Ways to encourage children's understanding, enjoyment and care of the natural world, especially city children.

Rainbow Colours.
A source of children's energy and contentment

(for teachers as well as parents)

Sharing knowledge about daylight and darkness and the physical and psychological effects of different colours. Using this knowledge to help children's concentration, composure and happiness and to reduce their feelings of threat and helplessness.

The Circle of Life. *Storytelling – Creation – Everything connects*

(for teachers as well as parents)
Helping children to explore ideas about the world and to find their place in it. The importance of storytelling.

Helping your Child with Yoga. *Balance, suppleness and self-respect*

(for teachers as well as parents)
Ancient wisdom about the mind, body and spirit translated for children. The story of Yoga. Stretching exercises. Introducing yoga postures to children. Energy for life, through self-confidence and self-control.

Stillness, Imagination and Meditation for Children.

(for teachers as well as parents)
Ways to help children get in touch with their own spirit and soul and realise their own power to love, to give comfort and to create beauty. Healing through meditation and art.

Inside Out. *Sharing disablement with each other.*

(for teachers as well as parents)
Strategies for understanding disablement and for sharing and giving support. Helping children over the fear and uncertainty barrier. Encouraging inventiveness and adventure. Disabled children from Uganda and Chailey Heritage in the U.K. tell their own stories.

Your Life. My Life.

(A book for 8–10 year olds for teachers as well as parents to use)
An introduction to human rights and human wrongs. Children's ideas. Inner freedom and outer freedom. Stories told, in their own words, by a street child in Calcutta, a Tibetan child escaping to Northern India and an El Salvadorian child living as a refugee in Guatemala.

Each of the **Right from the Start** books will be published as soon as funds become available to do so.

Feedback invitation

Each **Right from the Start** book provides a central starting point for the sharing of special or outstanding ways of caring for children that can make for calmer, happier and easier parenting and teaching. This will bring out the best in our children, whatever the circumstances in which we live.

This sharing has been a gift to the project from many people who love and care for children. So also have the funds raised from many sources towards each book's publication. Further fundraising will ensure that we can complete the project, continue working to improve, enrich and update the books and keep abreast of the changes taking place in society.

If your own experiences or understanding seem to be relevant and you feel you have valuable insights or experience to offer towards improving this book please write to:

Right from the Start. Feedback
c/o WAVE Trust, Cameron House
61 Friends Road, Croydon CR0 1ED
e-mail: wavetrust@aol.com

Sharing your responses to children will support us in our work to help them shine and protect them from harmful influences, increasing the confidence and encouragement that this series of books is able to give.

WAVE (Worldwide Alternatives to ViolencE) was founded in 1996 to research the causes of violence – especially child abuse – and promote effective means to reduce it. WAVE is working in partnership with Right from the Start towards a more peaceful society.

About the author

After reading Social Sciences at Exeter University and working with children on probation, Sarah Woodhouse became a Home Tutor for the Rugby Education Authority, teaching secondary school children who had been excluded from school. She also worked with the NSPCC during the 1970s when they were setting up special playgroups for mothers and their 'at risk' children. Sarah has been closely involved with special needs children for 23 years, and developed swimming, rowing and riding projects through a Saturday Club for physically and mentally disabled children under the age of 13.

She was the lead author of the first Amnesty International Education Pack for secondary schools, called *Teaching and Learning about Human Rights*. Subsequently she set up a charitable company called Right from the Start and, in collaboration with many other people, began researching, planning and writing this series of books for parents, carers and teachers.

Sarah has been married for 44 years. Her husband was the Head of Rugby School and later of Lancing College. In her role as a Headmaster's wife she has had many years of experience with children of all ages and their parents, and contact with many teachers.

Sarah and her husband have 4 children and 10 grandchildren. They live in Norfolk and have a small boat on the west coast of Scotland.

Ordering books

For further information or a book catalogue, please contact:

Hawthorn Press, 1 Lansdown Lane, Stroud, Gloucestershire GL5 1BJ
Tel: (01453) 757040   Fax: (01453) 751138   E-mail: info@hawthornpress.com
Website: www.hawthornpress.com

If you have difficulties ordering books from a bookshop, you can order direct from:

Booksource, 32 Finlas Street, Glasgow G22 5DU
Tel: (08702) 402182   Fax: (0141) 557 0189   E-mail: orders@booksource.net

or you can order online at **www.hawthornpress.com**